ANTIQUES
& COLLECTABLES
The Facts At Your Fingertips

ANTIQUES
& COLLECTABLES
The Facts At Your Fingertips

Introduction by

Judith Miller

Miller's Antiques and Collectables
The Facts at Your Fingertips

First published in Great Britain in 1993 by Miller's,
a division of Mitchell Beazley,
imprints of Octopus Publishing Group Ltd
2-4 Heron Quays
London E14 4JP

Copyright © Octopus Publishing Group Ltd 1993

Reprinted 1993, 1995, 1996, 1997
Revised edition 2000

Miller's is a registered trademark of Octopus Publishing Group Ltd

Editor Janet Gleeson
Art Editor Prue Bucknall
Special Photography Jacqui Hurst
Executive Art Editor John Grain
Production Fiona Wright
Indexer Hilary Bird
Art Director Tim Foster
Senior Executive Editor Frances Gertler

A CIP catalogue record for this book is available from the British Library
ISBN 1 84000 311 1

Set in Bembo
Typeset by SX Composing Ltd, Rayleigh, Essex
Origination by Scantrans Pte. Ltd, Singapore
Produced by Toppan (HK) Ltd
Printed in Hong Kong

Jacket*: A Kestner & Co. "Kewpie" doll, 1910; a Shelley "Vogue" cup and saucer, *c.*1930–33; a French brass framed carriage clock, *c.*1900; Marc Bolan's Gibson "Flying V" electric guitar, 1964 Model, *c.*1967/8; a 19thC Baccarat glass jug; an Irish yew table, *c.*1880; "Cheeky" a Merrythought teddy bear, 1957; a Kigu "Flying Saucer" musical powder compact, 1951.
Picture Pages 2 & 3: a 19thC William de Morgan two-handled vase; William IV silver gilt dessert-spoons; 18thC Meissen porcelain figures; a Baccarat rose paper-weight; an 18thC mahogany longcase clock by Samuel Guy; a pair of ruby slippers worn by Judy Garland; a 19thC French bracket clock; a Moorcroft baluster vase *c.*1928; a 19thC Staffordshire pottery Toby Jug; an early 19thC yew arm-chair; a George III soup tureen and cover *c.*1700; an 18thC mahogany bureau; a 19thC Kazak rug; a Meissen slop bowl, *c.*1730; two gauge 0 electric locomotives with pick-ups, *c.*1940; a Jules Steiner bisque doll, *c.*1890; a silver caster by Matthew Cooper, *c.*1703; a 17thC oak joint stool; a two-colour opaque twist wine glass *c.*1765.

CONTENTS

INTRODUCTION

People become interested in antiques and collectables for a variety of reasons. In my own case there was nothing in my background to suggest that I would – my parents had none. Indeed, my mother was of a generation which, for the most part, used to discard everything once it was old. However, as an impoverished student living in a run-down part of Edinburgh during the late 1960s I bought a few cheap, pretty plates from the local junk shops that I passed every day on my way to and from the university. To me they provided a far more attractive and unusual means of decorating the walls of my room than the posters favoured by my flatmates. In much the same way as many other people who inherit or buy the odd item of china or furniture, I then became increasingly intrigued as to when and where the plates had been made. Later still, I also became interested in their value. Were they now worth much more than I paid for them?

While my first foray into the world of antiques did not realize any profit to speak of, this in no way detracted from the considerable enjoyment my purchases gave me. Indeed, over the subsequent years, almost every collector I have met has bought for pleasure rather than profit; the value of any particular piece usually being a side issue to the joys of researching it, tracking it down, buying it, holding or looking at it, showing it off and even the simple fact of owning it.

Nevertheless, during a period in which buying and selling shares on the stock market has sometimes been a bit like swapping deck chairs on the *Titanic*, antiques and collectables have, for the most part, proved to be a good investment. This is undoubtedly one of the main reasons for the enormous ground swell of interest in the subject over the last decade. Moreover, the prospect of finding a long-forgotten object gathering dust in the attic, or buying for a few pounds an insignificant-looking item at a car boot sale that at auction turns out to be worth a small fortune, lends to this fascinating leisure activity all the excitement of a treasure hunt.

People often ask me how they can learn about antiques. Although there is no magic way of becoming an expert overnight, there's no great mystery to it either. Learning about antiques is great fun and the best way of going about it is to do what I did: visit museums and stately homes, read books and attend courses on the subject, look around antiques shops, markets, fairs and auctions and, above all, ask questions.

Museums and stately homes are a great place to start. Invariably they contain some of the finest examples of all manner of antiques and thus help you to get your eye in and learn when a piece looks right. However, don't try and take in too much at once. You'll learn far more quickly if you concentrate on one subject at a time.

There are also lots of books on antiques and collectables available today – many more than when I first became interested. *The Miller's Price Guides* and *Checklists*, for example, are particularly useful! Containing thousands of pictures of antiques they give you a pretty good idea of current prices and help to familiarize you with the language of antiques. Adult education courses run by leading auctioneers, such as Christie's and Sotheby's, or local education departments are also now widely available and offer expert tuition in a particular subject. If you do decide to attend one, don't feel embarrassed about asking questions. I remember attending a weekend course on porcelain run by Geoffrey Godden a few years ago. Right at the end a man suddenly confessed he had been confused by much of what had been said over the two days; he didn't understand the continual references to hard- and soft-paste porcelain, or what the difference was between them – a crucial piece of information that could have easily been explained if only he had asked at the outset.

Many people also feel intimidated about striking up a conversation with a dealer when visiting a shop, antiques fair or market. However, as I have found over the years, this is one of the best ways of acquiring knowledge. Indeed, most dealers are only too happy to discuss a piece and answer a reasonable number of questions. But do be sensitive to the fact that dealers have to make a living. Pick a quiet moment when they're not busy.

Attending auctions, which are held once a week or fortnight in most parts of the country, gives you the opportunity to view an enormous range of antiques and also introduces you to the real nitty-gritty of buying and selling. Go to the sale previews, buy a catalogue and, if you are particularly interested in a piece, ask to see someone from the auction house and discuss factors such as its history, any damage and the estimated price. Also go along to the sale itself, even if you have no intention of buying, and write down on the catalogue the prices pieces fetch as they go under the hammer. By doing this you will be able to compare estimates with realized prices, and gradually build up a feel for how the market is doing in particular areas.

By the time you have done all or most of the above you will have acquired a considerable amount of knowledge about the antiques you have become interested in. However, do bear in mind that we are not talking about an exact science here. For every rule there is an exception. For example, I once wrote an article confidently stating that all 18th-century sideboards had six legs. When this appeared in print it was accompanied by a number of illustrations, one of which showed a totally authentic piece with four legs! I have also heard three eminent experts in their field disagree vehemently over the authenticity of a piece of oak furniture. This is not an unusual occurrence and is very much part of the joy of antiques.

On a slightly more serious note, I've also seen so-called "antique" furniture made up by modern craftsmen using old wood and traditional techniques. Some pieces are so well done it's virtually impossible to distinguish between the fake and an original. As someone pointed out to me: there are more English oak refectory tables distributed around the world than there were houses in 16th-century England of a sufficient size to even get them in the front door. So do be careful, especially if you are thinking of paying a considerable amount of money for something. Most antiques dealers are both honest and honourable, but as is the case in most spheres of business, there are exceptions.

The questions I am most often asked are: how much is something worth, or how much should I pay for it? Well, price is almost always determined by a combination of four factors: condition, age, rarity and desirability. Condition can be vital. After a pristine Steiff teddy bear went for £55,000 at Sotheby's a few years ago, Bond Street was inundated with gentlemen in pinstripe suits clutching their play-worn childhood companions. There was considerable disappointment when they were informed that they were, at best, only worth £50–£100. Age is also obviously important, as the older something is the greater the likelihood few examples will have survived. However, the rarity of a piece does not guarantee desirability, and it is the latter that is the most important factor in determining the price something will fetch. For example, Roman glass is certainly old, can be found in good condition and some pieces are quite rare. However, if it is not considered desirable it will sell for a very low price at auction. In other words, the old adage that a piece is only worth what two people are prepared to pay for it usually holds good.

Assessing the value of an antique or a collectable is more difficult in some areas than others. For example, a good-quality 19th century mahogany dining table with chairs by a well-known maker can be said to have an intrinsic value. Precedent says they will at least have held their value 10 years on. Much the same can be said for pieces of 18th century porcelain or silverware. However, it is far more difficult to predict whether a 1950s Japanese plastic robot, a smashed-up Fender guitar once played by Jimi Hendrix (about ten years ago one fetched £35,000 at auction) or a Jean Paul Gaultier dress designed for Madonna will be worth in 30 years' time the sort of sums of money the present generation are prepared to pay for them. Of course, trying to predict these things is very much part of the fun of collecting – provided, that is, you stick to the following rules: always buy the best piece you can afford, especially in terms of condition and rarity. Never buy anything you don't like or you can't live with – you may have to live with it for a long time before you can get your money back. In fact, as long as you know what you're buying and the price you pay is appropriate at the time, you probably won't go far wrong.

JUDITH MILLER

PERIODS AND STYLES

DATES	BRITISH MONARCH	UK PERIOD	FRENCH PERIOD	GERMAN PERIOD	US PERIOD	STYLE
1558–1603	Elizabeth I	Elizabethan	Renaissance	Renaissance (to c.1650)	Early Colonial	Gothic
1603–1625	James I	Jacobean				
1625–1649	Charles I	Caroleon	Louis XIII (1610–1643)			Baroque (c.1620–1700)
1649–1660	Commonwealth	Cromwellian	Louis XIV (1643–1715)	Renaissance/ Baroque (c.1650–1700)		
1660–1685	Charles II	Restoration				
1685–1689	James II	Restoration				
1689–1694	William & Mary				William & Mary	
1694–1702	William III	William III			Dutch Colonial	Rococo (c.1695–1760)
1702–1714	Anne	Queen Anne		Baroque (c.1700–1730)	Queen Anne	
1714–1727	George I	Early Georgian	Régence	(1715–1723)	Chippendale	
1727–1760	George II	Early Georgian	Louis XV (1723–1774)	Rococo		
1760–1811	George III	Late Georgian	Louix XVI (1774–1793) Directoire (1793–1799) Empire (1799–1815)	Neoclassicism (c.1760–1800) Empire (c.1800–1815)	Early Federal (1790–1810) American Directoire (1798–1804) American Empire (1804–1815)	Neoclassical (c.1755–1805) Empire (c.1799–1815)
1812–1820	George III	Regency	Restauration (1815–1830)	Biedermeier (c.1815–1848)	Later Federal (1810–1830)	Regency (c.1812–1930)
1820–1830	George IV	Regency				
1830–1837	William IV	William IV	Louis Philippe (1830–1848)	Revivale (c.1830–1880)		Eclectic (c.1830–1880)
1837–1901	Victoria	Victorian	2nd Empire (1848–1870) 3rd Republic (1871–1940)	Jugendstil (c.1880–1920)	Victorian Art Nouveau (c.1900–1920)	Arts & Crafts (1800–1900)
1901–1910	Edward VII	Edwardian				Art Nouveau (c.1900–1920)

PART 1

WHERE

TO BEGIN

ABOVE ROYAL DOULTON BUNNYKINS DICOVERED AT A CAR
BOOT SALE AND LATER SOLD FOR NEARLY £4,000.

LEFT PORTOBELLO ROAD MARKET, LONDON

AUCTIONS

Auctions are one of the most exciting ways in which to buy antiques. Here you will find almost every type of collectable; from objects worth millions, to boxes of bric-a-brac costing just a few pounds. But buying at auction is very different from buying in a shop or market, and can seem quite bewildering to anyone who has never visited a saleroom or bought in this way before. Auctions are not limited to the big city salerooms. The London branches of famous firms such as Sotheby's, Christie's, Phillips and Bonhams may account for the vast majority of more expensive antiques sold at auction in this country, but they also have provincial branches and there is a network of local auctioneers throughout the country where you can often buy less expensive antiques and bric-a-brac, provided you are willing to sift through the varied goods on offer to find whatever it is you are looking for.

Most would-be collectors who overcome their initial misgivings and visit an auction for the first time find themselves hooked on

---

> ## BUYING AT AUCTION
> - **BUY THE CATALOGUE**
> - **VIEW THE SALE VERY THOROUGHLY**
> - **DECIDE ON YOUR PRICE LIMIT AND STICK TO IT**

---

the exciting atmosphere of the saleroom. The large turnover of goods means that there is always a possibility of uncovering an undiscovered treasure – or "sleeper" as it is known in the trade – and provided certain basic guidelines are followed, auctions are still one of the best places to buy objects of good quality at a reasonable price.

Going to auctions regularly can also be an excellent way to learn about the area you are interested in before beginning to collect. If you attend saleroom previews regularly and read the auction catalogues carefully, you will soon acquire a sound knowledge and a feel for prices which will stand you in good stead when you begin to spend money on your collection.

BUYING AT AUCTION
CATALOGUES

Before every sale is held, the saleroom will identify the goods to be sold in a catalogue. Whether it's a typed sheet or a glossy illustrated publication, it will list and number the objects in the order in which they will be sold. The numbers in the catalogue, known as "lot" numbers, correspond to those attached to each object or "lot".

Next to each catalogue entry there may be a suggested price range, for example £50–80. These figures show the price the auction house valuer expects the object to fetch, and are known as the "estimate". If there are no estimates printed in the catalogue they may be pinned up in the saleroom; if not, ask the auctioneer. Estimates should only ever be taken as a rough guide; they are never a guarantee of the price for which something will be sold. Ultimately any work of art, no matter how

Some lots contain more than one item; all these albums were sold together in a stamp sale.

rare or valuable, is only worth at auction what two or more people are willing to bid for it, and it is this element of uncertainty that gives auctions their special appeal.

VIEWING THE SALE

About two or three days before the day of the sale, all the objects to be sold will be put on display, so that buyers can examine them; this is known as the "view" or "sale preview". If you are hoping to buy at the sale it is important to attend one of these preview days because on the morning of the sale, when the porters are getting everything ready for selling, it may be impossible to view properly.

At the preview you will notice that every object has been marked with its lot number which corresponds to the number in your catalogue. Objects are rarely displayed in numerical order, so if something sounded fascinating in the catalogue and you can't find it at the view, ask one of the saleroom staff to help you. That way you won't miss anything which has been badly displayed.

When at larger auction houses, pay careful attention to the exact wording of each catalogue entry. Read the explanations at the beginning of the catalogue, which tell you the significance of words such as "attributed to", "style of" and "after". This catalogue terminology is like a code which tells you the valuer's opinion of the date and authenticity of a piece and will have an important bearing on its value.

Above Each lot should be clearly marked with a number.
Right Viewing before the auction takes place.

Ask to speak to the expert in charge of the sale if you would like more information about a particular piece.

Always examine very, very thoroughly any object on which you intend to make a bid, and make up your own mind as to its authenticity. Pay particular attention to the condition of the piece and take into account the potential cost of restoration, which may be quite considerable, before deciding on your bidding limit. Also bear in mind that an auctioneer's commission (usually about 10–15% added on to the hammer price – the price at which the object is sold in the saleroom) and VAT on the commission, will usually be added to the hammer price.

BIDDING

If after viewing the sale, you decide you might want to bid, find out if you need to

(usually about 100) to work out roughly when your lot will be sold; but always remember to allow yourself a bit of extra time so you don't arrive too late.

If you can't get to the sale you can usually leave a bid with the commissions clerk, who will bid on your behalf.

When the sale begins, the auctioneer will call out each lot number to be sold and will start the bidding at a figure which is usually slightly below the lower estimate. As the people present signal to him by waving or nodding he will call out their bids in regular sums, called increments. Depending on the value of the piece, the bidding could rise in £5s, £10s, £20s, £100s, £1,000s, or more, the increments increasing as the price rises. The auctioneer will indicate that the bidding is finished by banging a small hammer, called a gavel, on the rostrum, and recording the sale and the name or number of the successful bidder. People who have never been to an auction before often worry that an ill-timed cough or sneeze could be mistaken as a bid and land them with a masterpiece; ask anyone with experience of auctions and they will tell you that this is unheard of.

When you are bidding for the first time remember to make your bids clearly and quickly. In a packed saleroom it can be quite difficult to attract the auctioneer's attention, so don't be faint-hearted: wave your catalogue or bidding card and call out if need be. However, if the bidding is rising rapidly and the auctioneer seems to be ignoring you, don't worry; an auctioneer will usually only take bids from two people at a time; when one drops out he will look around the room for someone else to join in. If you are still within your limit that is your moment!

An auction of silver in progress.

register first. Some salerooms will want you to fill in a form with your name, address and phone number before the sale; some issue you with a number to hold up should your bid be successful; in others you simply call out your name and fill in a form at the time.

If you are not paying in cash, ask before the sale whether a cheque or credit card will be acceptable as a method of payment. If you intend to spend a large sum of money you may have to supply bank references.

Some sales last for several hours; if the lots which interest you are towards the end of the sale and you don't want to sit through the whole auction, find out how many lots the auctioneer expects to sell per hour

SELLING AT AUCTION

Taking a prized possession for sale at auction can seem every bit as daunting as buying, especially if you don't know the object's history or what it might be worth. You are, after all, taking along something you hope may be valuable, and quite possibly have treasured for a very long time. But although many would-be vendors are put off by the thought of rejection, auction houses actually offer a very useful way of finding out more about your property and their advice is nearly always absolutely free.

WHAT IT'S WORTH

When you are visiting one of the larger auction houses you will probably have to queue up and show your property to a receptionist who will decide which expert should be called to value it for you.

Before the auction-house expert examines your property he (or she) will probably ask you for anything you can tell him about the object. The history of an object, known as its "provenance", can help enormously in its correct identification and valuation. Even details which might seem insignificant to you can help a valuer, so if you know your table once belonged to Aunt Ethel who lived in Devon and bought it from a local Duchess, then don't forget to say so.

After careful examination the valuer will probably tell you what he can about your object. This may be where, when and by whom it was made, as well as what he thinks it might fetch at auction.

Should you decide to sell, the valuer should also advise you whether a "reserve" price is necessary. A reserve is the minimum price for which the auctioneer may sell your property, and can act as an important safeguard if the sale turns out to be very

> ## SELLING AT AUCTION
> - TRY TO GET MORE THAN ONE VALUER'S OPINION
> - PHONE TO MAKE AN APPOINTMENT IF NECESSARY
> - AGREE ALL CHARGES BEFORE LEAVING YOUR PROPERTY FOR SALE
> - FIND OUT HOW SOON YOUR PROPERTY WILL APPEAR AT AUCTION

poorly attended. You should also remember to ask the valuer how quickly your property will be sold. If the property is of exceptional quality you may be advised to wait for a particular sale which will feature other high-quality objects and attract better prices. Certain specialist sales are only held once or twice a year, and it may be that you could sell your property more quickly elsewhere.

THE COST OF SELLING

An auction house does not buy your property from you, instead it sells on your behalf. For this service you will be charged a commission (usually about 10–15% deducted from the hammer price), VAT on the commission and costs, such as an insurance charge and a handling charge. If your item is illustrated in the catalogue you may also be charged a fee to cover the photographic costs. Finally, in the unlikely event that your property remains unsold there may be other charges, albeit reduced.

An auction-house expert giving an over-the-counter valuation.

ANTIQUES SHOPS

Antiques shops are among the easiest of places in which to begin learning about and buying antiques. They are less frantic than auction rooms, you can buy when you feel like it, and you don't have to compete with anyone else for the object of your choice.

There is an enormous variety of antiques shops, from the smart West End galleries to small country and local dealers. Obviously the dealer you choose will be determined to some extent by personal taste and how much money you have to spend. But as in any trade there are disreputable dealers as well as honest ones, and, particularly if you are an inexperienced buyer, it is very important to pick a dealer who is both knowledgeable and trustworthy.

One of the best ways to find a reputable dealer is through trade associations like the BADA and LAPADA (see p165). You can phone these organizations and ask for lists of local member dealers to be sent to you,

Below The Lanes, Brighton, Sussex.
Right A general antiques shop, Brighton

free of charge. If, on the other hand, you are wandering down your high street and about to enter a tantalizing shop, remember to look in the window or on the door first; a trade association sign is a good indication that the dealer has stock of good quality and also knows his subject.

In Britain the two major trade associations are the LAPADA and BADA (the equivalent American bodies are the AADLA and NAADA). Those dealers who wish to become members of these bodies have to undergo a very rigorous selection procedure. This assesses both their stock and knowledge. Once members they are bound to keep to a strict code of practice which offers you, as a buyer, reassuring protection, especially if you are about to purchase something costly for the first time. Member dealers are bound to tell you as much about the piece as they can; and this includes pointing out any restoration the piece may have had. If after buying something from a member dealer, you discover it is not genuine, the organization will themselves organize a panel of independent experts to investigate your claim and make sure, if it is upheld, that you get a full and speedy refund. Remember that even the best-intentioned dealers can make the odd genuine mistake. But a good dealer will want you to come back so it's not in their interests to "do" you.

The ideal antiques shop should not only be reputable, it should also have a welcoming atmosphere in which you do not feel intimidated or pressurized to buy. It is worth returning to a dealer you trust because as you build up a rapport he will

---

BUYING FROM ANTIQUES SHOPS

- PICK A REPUTABLE DEALER
- TAKE YOUR TIME WHEN DECIDING WHAT TO BUY
- GET A DETAILED RECEIPT

LAPADA

houses, to make sure the price is a fair one. It is almost expected to ask the dealer whether the price he first mentions is his "best" one. Don't feel embarrassed to do this, most are quite happy to haggle and will come down a little – one well-known London dealer even takes buyers to task if they don't ask for a discount!

Before you make your final decision, ask the dealer as many questions as possible about the piece. Find out how old it is, whether it's marked, what it's made from, who made it, where, and whether it has been restored.

If you decide to buy the piece, make sure you are given a full written receipt, which states the dealer's name, address and telephone number, together with the date the piece was made, a full description of it, the price you have paid, and the date of the purchase. It is very important to keep this receipt in a safe place. You will need it for insurance or in the unlikely event that the piece turns out not to be genuine.

probably be able to help you in a variety of other ways. He might let you take things home "on approval". He may operate a "buy back" scheme, which means he will let you sell back to him the objects your bought from him for the price you paid for them (a useful way of upgrading your collection). He may also look out for special things to add to your collection, and give advice and condition reports on objects you have seen at auction. Above all, a friendly dealer is one of the best ways of learning, from the inside, about your chosen subject and the fascinating world of antiques.

BUYING FROM ANTIQUES SHOPS

Unlike buying at auction, there is no pressure to buy at a particular moment from a dealer, and this gives you plenty of time to decide whether you really want the object.

Before buying any antique do try to price similar pieces at other shops or auction

JUNK SHOPS

The contents of many junk shops come from house clearance sales and deceased properties where the entire contents were bought for a fixed sum. Thus you will probably find an enormous variety of different types of objects all for sale, usually for relatively inexpensive prices. Most of the items for sale in a junk shop will not be "antiques", but they are a good place to look for early 20th century furniture and decorative items. Buying from a junk shop is rather different from buying from an antiques shop, because you must decide for yourself on the age, value and authenticity of a piece. Nonetheless, if you have a keen eye, they can be a fruitful source of inexpensive collectables and a trawl through dusty boxes may reveal an unexpected bargain. As always, be ready to haggle and remember to ask for a receipt.

SELLING TO AN ANTIQUES SHOP

Contrary to popular belief it is not always best to sell at auction. Selling to an antique shop has numerous advantages. Once you have reached an agreement with a dealer in an antiques shop, you will probably be paid as soon as you hand over your property, and there will probably be no hidden deductions for commission, insurance etc. (see p28). Selling to a dealer saves waiting for the sale which may be several weeks away and waiting for payment after the sale (usually at least two weeks).

Before selling to a dealer, however, you do need to be sure of the value of your property. The public nature of auction sales means that objects of value should always realize their potential value, even if the auction-house valuer has underestimated them. In selling to a dealer you have no such safeguard; you get the

> ### SELLING TO ANTIQUES SHOPS
> - FIND OUT WHICH SHOPS SPECIALIZE IN YOUR TYPE OF PROPERTY
> - TRY TO GET MORE THAN ONE OFFER BEFORE SELLING
> - NEVER SELL TO ANYONE WHO TURNS UP UNINVITED AT YOUR HOME

price you agree, no more and no less.

Do a little research before offering your property for sale and find out which dealers specialize in the type of object you are offering. You are far more likely to be quoted a fair price for a Victorian chair if you take it to a dealer in 19th century furniture, than if you show it to an 18th century specialist.

If your property is too large or difficult to take to the dealer's shop, many are very happy to visit you in your home, although do make sure you pick a reputable one (see p16) before inviting him in.

There is an old adage about dealers with more than a little truth in it: if there were four dealers and one Chippendale chair on an island, all the dealers would make a living! Don't be surprised if you are offered a wide range of prices for your property as you do the rounds with it. A dealer's offer will, to some extent, be dependent on what he thinks he can sell it on for, and remember he has to make a profit or he would not be in business.

Opposite An antiques emporium, Portobello Road, London.
Below A variety of decorative 19th and 20th century ceramics for sale.

KNOCKERS

Never open your door to any "dealer" who calls uninvited, or who puts a note through your door telling you that they will pay cash for valuables and will return a day or two later. Many of these so called "knockers" are of very dubious integrity and their aim is to trick owners, particularly the elderly and vulnerable, into selling their property for much less than its true value. There is also the added risk of allowing into your home an unknown person, who may well be using the visit as an opportunity to plan to return later without an invitation.

ANTIQUES FAIRS & MARKETS

Visiting antiques markets and fairs is a fairly effortless way of seeing a large number of dealers together and gives you a useful opportunity to compare their stock, and its quality and price. You can find out where and when they are held from local papers and antiques magazines. There are several different types of antiques markets and fairs:

- Large "vetted" fairs – where dealers from all over the country take stands and every exhibit is checked to make sure it is genuine.
- Fairs where the objects are not checked and anyone can take a stand.
- Permanent markets where specialist dealers congregate with shops and stalls every day, or several days a week.
- Weekly street markets where small traders sell goods from the early hours of the morning to other dealers, as well as the general public.

VETTED FAIRS

At a large antiques fair you will probably have to pay an admission charge; for this you may be given a catalogue to the fair which lists the various dealers exhibiting and their specialities; if not, such catalogues will usually be available to buy. Many of the larger fairs which are held on a regular basis protect buyers by "vetting" all the exhibitors and their stock. This means that before the fair opens, a panel of experts on each subject will examine items for sale on each stand to make sure they are authentic. At the best fairs, the vetting is an extremely rigorous procedure and even the most eminent dealers have been known to quake with anticipation at the arrival of the panel on their stand!

Most larger fairs operate a "dateline", which means that only objects made before a certain date may be exhibited at the fair. The datelines will usually be mentioned in the catalogue, but they may vary for

The British International Antiques Fair at the National Exhibition Centre, Birmingham.

different types of collectable. For example, pre-1900 for furniture, but pre-1930 for ceramics and pictures.

Large fairs usually feature a wide variety of different types of collectables, so you will find furniture, silver, ceramics, jewellery, textiles and much more besides, under one roof. There are also annual specialist fairs which focus on one particular collecting area: silver, ceramics, and even dolls all have their specialist fairs. If you are a keen collector such events can offer a golden opportunity to meet leading authorities in their field, who may come from other distant parts of the country and otherwise be difficult to visit.

If you find yourself bemused by the bustle of the fair, don't be afraid to ask for a dealer's card, and arrange to visit them at their premises after the event. Dealers view fairs as a place to meet new collectors and forge new contacts, as well as make sales.

OTHER FAIRS

There is a world of difference between the large vetted fairs, and the plethora of smaller "antiques" fairs which are held up and down the country in church halls, schools and other similar venues. There you may still be charged an entrance fee, but there will probably be no catalogue, and no dateline or vetting, of the goods on offer. Many of the objects for sale may be better described as second-hand rather than antique, but nevertheless, provided you realize that you must satisfy yourself of the authenticity of anything you buy, such events can prove entertaining for a browse, and are sometimes a good place to buy inexpensive bric-a-brac and decorative items – and you may even find a bargain.

MARKETS

Throughout the various antiques centres in Britain there are many permanent antiques markets where several traders have stalls

Portobello Road, London.

under one roof, or in a particular street (see p164). In London there are a variety of different types of market, many of which (Portobello Road, for example), have become famous tourist attractions, as well as being busy antiques markets.

Highly reputable specialist dealers, many of them members of trade associations, often choose to operate from large permanent antiques markets. Visiting such markets can be a good way of discovering dealers who specialize in particularly unusual types of collectables, and the goods on offer will usually be fairly priced. Since, unlike a non-specialist who may be inclined to over-value an object with which he is not familiar, a specialist will know precisely what it is worth and will be competitive with other local traders.

Throughout the country, and especially in London, there are also weekly markets where you can buy antiques. One of the largest and most fascinating is held in Bermondsey in the East End of London from 5am every Friday morning. Here traders buy and sell to one another, as well as to private collectors, and provided you are confident enough in your particular field of interest, such markets can be wonderful sources of bargains, but you usually need to get there early to find the best buys.

SELLING AT FAIRS AND MARKETS

If you have a considerable quantity of suitable goods to sell you might want to take a stand in a local antiques fair. You can find out how to set about this from the fair organizers. Hiring a stand will probably involve a deposit or payment up front and there may be a waiting list if competition for spaces is fierce. If you only have a few pieces, you could try selling them direct to a

Bustling London market stalls at Bermondsey (above left) and Portobello Road (top and right).

BUYING FROM
FAIRS AND MARKETS

Whatever type of fair or market you attend, if you decide to buy, always make sure you get a written receipt, with the dealer's name and address and a description of your purchase on it (see p16).

market trader. To sell in this way, pick a stand where they sell objects similar to yours. Go early and, when the market is quiet, approach the trader. If you don't manage to sell at the first stand, make sure you pack your treasures carefully before you go on to the next stall.

CAR BOOT SALES

A few years ago, a buyer at a car boot sale spotted some appealing pottery rabbits and bought them for a few pounds (see illustration on p11). The new owner then took her bunnies along to an auction house for an expert opinion. They were immediately identified as being rare early examples of Royal Doulton's Bunnykins series and sold soon after for nearly £4,000. Such stories are not everyday occurrences, but the mere fact that they happen at all has helped ensure the growing appeal of the car boot sale.

Car boot sales are held in a wide variety of venues, usually fields, school playgrounds or car parks. They may be advertized in the classified columns of certain magazines, local papers, or simply by notices pinned up in your area. Some are regular events, held every Sunday, others are "one-offs", or held only occasionally.

The boot sale is a good way of emptying the contents of your loft or garage, and raising some cash for your collection. For a small admission charge anyone can fill their car with their unwanted property and sell it for whatever they can. You can buy and sell almost anything at a boot sale – old furniture, second-hand clothes, books, electrical equipment and much more besides. If you are a collector of modest means, boot sales provide an ideal opportunity to buy relatively inexpensive collectables, but you have to be determined enough to sift through the heaps of uninteresting objects to find the tantalizing but elusive treasures.

Vintage cameras at a car boot sale.

BUYING AT A BOOT SALE

If you are about to visit a car boot sale for the first time there are a few simple guidelines which could help make your day more successful.

Firstly, remember to arrive early - very early. This way you will be able to get the pick of the items on offer and will be more likely to spot any bargains before they can be snapped up by someone else. If it's wintertime, take a torch with you; you'll need it to see what's on offer in the poor light. You should also remember to take plenty of cash, preferably in coins and small notes. You can't expect people at a boot sale to welcome cheques, nor to have unlimited amounts of change available. Keep your cash in a purse belt or something similar, not only for the sake of security, but also because this will leave your hands free to examine the goodies!

If you do see something which takes your fancy, ask its price, but feel free to haggle over it. Bear in mind that there are no fixed prices at a boot sale; the objects on offer are only worth what someone is willing to pay for them.

SELLING AT A BOOT SALE

Careful planning and preparation are the key to successful selling at a boot sale. Work out what you are taking, and whether it will all fit in your car. Remember to allow extra space for a table, to display your property (a wall-papering table or picnic table would be ideal) and a collapsible chair to sit on. When you pack the car, try to pack the table on top, so that you don't have to unload everything on to the ground before being able to get the table out.

If you want to price things, do so clearly with sticky labels or tickets. Put on the price you would ideally like to receive, but be prepared to come down a little from this figure if need be. Remember to pack anything fragile with plenty of wrapping: newspaper and cardboard boxes are best for china and glass, etc. Old blankets are useful for wrapping round pictures and prints.

Wear suitable clothes: rainwear and boots are often a good idea if the sale is in a muddy field. Take some sandwiches and a thermos of tea or coffee so you are well prepared for your day. Allow plenty of time for the journey, and try to arrive early so you can get a good position where the maximum number of buyers will spot your goods early on, before they have spent all their money somewhere else. Don't be surprised if dealers start to rummage in your boot while you're unpacking – it can be disconcerting but it's also a good way to "break the ice"! Try and take plenty of spare change with you (keep it safe in a purse belt), and avoid accepting cheques whenever possible.

Finally, before the sale is over, try and arrange for a friend to come and help you. That will give you a chance to take a break and look at what everyone else has to offer, and maybe spend some of your earnings at the same time.

Bargain-hunting at a boot sale.

ADVERTS

Private advertisements are an alternative way of buying and selling antiques. You may find advertisements for antiques in a wide variety of publications, from national newspapers to specialist magazines.

One of the main worries with buying and selling through adverts is the danger to your personal safety, and the security of your property. However, provided you take the necessary precautions to minimize risks, this can be an effective way of buying and selling antiques.

BUYING FROM ADVERTS

If you're responding to an advertisement in a newspaper or magazine, try and find out as much as possible about the piece before you go and see it. Ask how big it is, what sort of condition it is in and the price.

If after all this you are still interested in the piece, make an appointment to go and see it. Find out the vendor's name as well as the address, and the home phone number if this is not the one in the advertisement. Try to go with someone else; if you must go alone, tell someone where you are going, including the name, address and phone number of the person, and when you expect to be back.

When you see the piece, remember to examine it very thoroughly for damage and restoration before making up your own mind as to its age and authenticity. If you decide to buy it, or if you have to leave a deposit, remember to ask for a written receipt, which includes the name and address of the person you are buying from and the date.

SELLING THROUGH ADVERTS

Adverts can be a good way of selling your property if you don't want to sell through a dealer or at an auction, but first you must decide where to place your advert and how much your property is worth.

Your choice of publication will probably be dictated by both your budget and the value and type of your property. Look for a publication which has a large number of objects of a similar sort to yours. If the object you are selling might be of interest to a particular type of collector, look at the specialist collectors' magazines, as these are usually relatively inexpensive to advertise in and will reach a wider audience of potential buyers than a more general publication. If, for examplem, you are selling an old doll, you might well be more successful if you advertise in a doll collector's magazine, rather than in your local paper. Once you have narrowed down the field of possible publications, you could even try phoning the numbers in one or two similar advertisements to see what sort of response they have had.

Before you place the advertisement, find out what your property is worth. Show the object to a few reputable dealers, or take it to an auction house to get a good idea of what you could reasonably ask for it.

Word the advertisement clearly and succinctly; try to mention the age of the piece if you know it. You can either give a box number or your phone number for interested buyers to respond to, but don't mention your name and address because this might encourage burglars.

If you have given a telephone number, try to be in to take calls when the publication first appears, and be prepared to give callers a full description over the phone (writing this out beforehand will make your life easier). It is quite a good idea to take a deposit from anyone who says they want to buy the object but will come back at a later date to pay and collect it. That way you will ensure you do get paid and will not lose out on other potential buyers who may respond to your advertisement. Try to avoid cheques; cash or a banker's order are much safer.

PART 2

BRINGING IT HOME

ABOVE UNWRAPPING A 19TH CENTURY
CARRIAGE CLOCK.

LEFT PORCELAIN DISPLAYED IN PURPOSE–BUILT
CABINETS

VALUING & INSURING

No keen collector enjoys contemplating the thought of losing a prized possession, but unfortunately, an unpleasant aspect of collecting antiques today is the growing risk of burglary. One result of the increasing number of art and antiques thefts is that the majority of insurance companies now demand a full, professionally written, valuation to cover objects worth more than a certain amount.

If you are beginning to buy antiques you will certainly know what each piece is worth, and whether you need a valuation. But supposing you bought them a decade or more ago, or have been given or inherited them, do you really know what they're worth, and for what sums they should be insured? In recent years, many types of antiques have risen dramatically in value. Numerous, once modestly valued objects are now worth substantial sums, so if you are unsure about the value of your collection, and whether you need a valuation, it is always a good idea to take professional advice. Remember, although a valuation will involve some expense, if you don't have your possessions valued you could find that in the event of burglary or accident you are inadequately insured and as a result are unable to replace your property.

VALUATIONS

There are various ways of having your antiques valued. If you know a friendly local dealer, and only have a few items, they may be able to provide you with a valuation, although you should check with your insurance company that this will be acceptable. If you have a fairly extensive collection, your insurance company may prefer a valuation from a specialist valuer, or one of the larger auction houses, all of whom have large valuation departments.

One of the main advantages in using an auction house is that although most of the valuing will be done by "generalists" (valuers with experience in assessing many different types of antiques), if there is anything unusual in your collection, or anything they are unsure of, they can call

Opposite A Japanese cloisonné vase c.1910, discovered by one of Bonham's insurance valuers. Its owner thought it was worth around £2,000. The vase was identified as the work of one of Japan's most prominent cloisonné craftsmen, Kyoto Namikawa, and later sold for over £60,000.

Below Valuation documents are required by increasing numbers of insurance companies.

upon specialist experts for advice. Every year an amazing number of valuable treasures come to light when auction-house valuers visit collectors' homes. Among the most extraordinary finds of recent years are a priceless Ming bowl being used for a dog's water, and a medieval bronze employed as a door stop! Both of these were later sold for several thousand pounds.

THE COST OF VALUING

Before you decide who to call in to value your property, do shop around and look for the best deal. Prices for valuations vary, and can be calculated in various ways, either as a percentage of the total value of your property (usually between ½% and 1½%), on a daily rate, or as an agreed flat rate. As a general guide, a valuer will be able to assess between 100–300 pieces per day. To some extent the fee you are quoted for your valuation will depend upon how much the auction house wishes to secure you as a client. To an auction house, a valuation is recognized as being an important way of establishing loyalty with their firm. So the chances are that if you have an unusually extensive collection of, say, Dinkies, the auction house will be keen to lure you to their firm, and may be prepared to negotiate. You should always make sure you agree the final figure before the valuation takes place, not afterwards. Some auction houses offer an added bonus by reducing their commission rates, should you decide to sell any of the items they have valued within a reasonably short period of time.

Whoever carries out your valuation, you should make sure it includes a full description of every item, together with its dimensions and a value for insurance purposes. The value placed upon each object will to some extent depend on where you would go to replace your property; would you go shopping in Bond Street, or at your local auction house? The price an insurance valuer puts on your property will probably be at least 20% higher than what you could expect to get should you decide to sell. If you feel that this will make your insurance premiums too high, you can opt for "market valuations" – in other words auction prices – instead. But bear in mind if the valuation is too low you could find yourself unable to replace lost items satisfactorily.

INSURING

The person you choose to value your antiques may be able to advise you on a suitable insurer. One way of reducing premiums is to shop around. If your collection is moderately large and valuable you will probably find it is less expensive to insure through a broker specializing in art and antiques, rather than through a large composite insurer. Whereas a large insurer will usually lump together your antiques as part of the general household policy, a specialist broker will assess the risk of different categories of antique individually, which will tend to reduce the premiums. The cost of insuring the different categories will vary, with large items like furniture often less expensive than particularly fragile pieces or small items like boxes, dolls and teddy bears and dressing-table silverware, which are easily portable and so incur a higher risk of theft.

SECURITY

There are two important ways in which you can protect your collection. Firstly, you should try to deter potential thieves from entering your home by making it as secure as possible. If you are unsure about how to go about this, you can contact the crime prevention officer through the local police station. He will be able to advise you on ways of safeguarding your belongings and should be able to recommend a reputable security firm in your area who can install additional locks or alarms or whatever other equipment may be necessary.

But what if disaster should strike, and you do find yourself the victim of crime? You can assist the recovery of the stolen property by marking your belongings with a security pen (available through the crime prevention officer), which only shows up under an ultraviolet light. However, many collectors prefer not to mark their antiques in this way, because the pen is indelible, and should you want to sell the item at a later date it could deter prospective buyers. By far the best way of helping the police to retrieve your possessions is by supplying them with as much information about your stolen property as possible. An inventory, or list of your collection, will be invaluable for this (see p31), but it is also vitally important to have a clear photograph of each object in your collection.

Photographs of any stolen antiques can be logged via your local police officer with the Art and Antiques Squad at Scotland Yard. This police department has a national database, which contains descriptions and photographic images of works of art stolen throughout the country. When stolen property is recovered, the Art and Antiques Squad can identify the rightful owner – provided the object has been logged on their computer system. But you do need a photograph to stand a good chance of success. It's salutary to remember that the vast majority of stolen antiques the police recover are never claimed. In such cases not only does the culprit evade prosecution, but the property in question is returned to him! By photographing all the items in your collection, you will help to redress this balance, and greatly increase the chances of recovering stolen items should you fall victim to crime.

> ## THE ART & ANTIQUES POLICE SQUAD'S TIPS
> - PHOTOGRAPH ITEMS AGAINST A PLAIN BACKGROUND (WHITE OR GREY IS USUALLY BEST)
> - TRY AND FILL THE VIEW FINDER WITH THE IMAGE
> - PUT A RULER BESIDE EACH OBJECT TO GIVE AN IDEA OF SCALE
> - PHOTOGRAPH MARKS, CHIPS, DENTS AND SCRATCHES

PHOTOGRAPHING

You may want to enlist the help of a professional photographer to photograph your collection, although if you observe a few simple guidelines it is quite a simple task to do it yourself. It is best to photograph objects using colour film outdoors in natural daylight. Choose a day when there's a light cloud cover, so the sunlight is not too harsh and the shadows aren't very noticeable. Standard 35mm 100 ASA print film, or a specially improved Polaroid camera are good options, although the older type of Polaroids, which are sometimes used by auction houses for research, are not generally useful as long term photographic records, because the colours can fade. For the clearest results the new digital cameras can be used. Many police stations have cameras available on loan, although you may have to supply the film. More details should be available from your local crime prevention officer.

To get the best results stand with the sun behind you, level with the object, not above or to the side, and close enough to fill the view finder. If the objects are very small, it is best to photograph them against a plain background; white is usually the best colour for this, unless the object itself is predominantly white, in which case use a grey or black background. It's also useful when photographing your collection to include a scale reference; a ruler placed beside each object is a good way of doing this. If the object is behind glass, stand slightly to one side to avoid unwanted reflections and glare.

Take at least one shot of each object, as well as close-up shots of any identifying scratches, bumps or marks on each piece. These detailed shots are especially important if the object is likely to be similar to many others. If you can show the crack on the ear of your Staffordshire dog, the hallmarks of your Victorian candlestick or the chip on the face of your carriage clock, they will provide an invaluable method of positive identification. As well as these individual photographs, it's also a good idea to take general shots of your room. These will help you to remember any smaller items which you may forget to list.

Remember to keep your photographs together in a safe place. Ideally, they should be filed in your inventory beside the entry for each object (see below). It's also a wise precaution to store a copy of photographs somewhere else for safekeeping; your bank or with your solicitor would be ideal.

DOCUMENTING

Documenting your collection means keeping a record of every collectable object as you acquire it. It's a good idea to keep your records of each item in your collection

all together in an inventory book. Then, as your collection grows, you will find you have a useful source of reference as well as an interesting reminder of how your collection began.

Keeping a detailed record of each object in your collection is also an ideal way to show proof of ownership in the event of an insurance claim. So any new purchase should be documented and photographed as soon as possible after you have brought it home.

When beginning an inventory of your collection first make a list of every object you wish to include. Then write down the following information for each object :

- Where it came from.
- The date you bought or acquired it.
- The price you paid for it.
- The value for insurance purposes if your collection is insured.
- A full description of the piece, including its size, what it is made from, and any decorative features.
- A report of its condition, including cracks, chips, alterations or restoration. This should be updated whenever you have the piece restored.
- Anything else you know about the object's history.

It is also a good idea to keep the receipts of any items you have purchased in the same place as the inventory.

A detailed inventory of your collection is invaluable when claiming against burglary or damage.

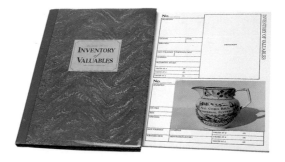

DISPLAY

Antiques can be displayed in a multitude of different ways, but it's important that the method you select should be appropriate to your lifestyle. You may long to display your collection of antiques throughout your home; however, if, for example, you have pets or children, fragile or potentially hazardous objects should probably be kept well out of harm's way – perhaps up on a shelf or out of reach in a cabinet Bear in mind that not only can children or pets damage vulnerable and valuable objects, but that antiques can also pose a threat to their safety. Even something as seemingly innocuous as an old teddy bear may contain wires that could harm a small child.

However, so long as you take simple precautions, there is no need to feel frightened of your collection. Many types of antiques, such as furniture, glass and silver, can still be used for their original purpose, or adapted for modern-day living. Successful display should allow you to enjoy your collection as much as possible, whilst still conserving it in good condition.

Before you decide where to position your antiques, you should bear in mind how the piece was originally intended to be seen and used. Some pieces of furniture, for instance, were made to be placed against a wall, others were meant to be centrally positioned; try and display the piece in an appropriate manner. If you have a smaller object, say a sculpture, which is meant to be seen in the round, and you have nowhere suitable to put it, you could place it in front of a mirror, so that it can still be appreciated from every angle.

You may find you need to have shelves or cupboards specially constructed to house your collection. However, before you decide where to install special fittings, don't forget that nearly all types of antiques, with the exception of ceramics, silver and other types of metalware, should be displayed away from strong sunlight and direct sources of heat (see p34). So don't, for instance, display your samplers in front of a sunny window, and try to keep the backs of antique furniture away from radiators. If your room is a particularly sunny one, objects such as textiles and prints can be displayed behind non-reflective, light-resistant glass, which will allow you to enjoy them whilst protecting them from fading. If you need to mount old photographs, or printed ephemera, in order to display them behind glass it is best to use mounting tape rather than glue, which can irreversibly damage the objects themselves.

Among the many aids to the effective display of collections of antiques are pedestals, stands and hangers. Most of these can be purchased through department and good hardware stores. Other specialized pieces of display equipment are available by mail order through specialist magazines.

If you have a collection of vases or plates, or glass, you may consider having a series of small brackets built to display them. Make sure, however, that they all sit securely on their perches. If you are displaying plates on brackets, they will need to be propped up on plate stands. Before climbing up to put them in their final resting place, it's a good idea to test them on their stands at an accessible height, so you can check they are firm and unlikely to roll off. Plates and ceramic flatwares can also be simply hung on a wall. The best method for this is to use an acrylic hanger: these are transparent, adjustable and have no sharp points to scratch the surface of the piece. For more robust types of ceramic modern plastic-coated wire and spring plate hangers are also suitable. These come in a wide variety of sizes, so make sure you choose the right one. If it's too small it could put the plate under strain and cause it to crack, and if it's too large the plate could fall down. To check the size is right put the hanger on top of the rack; it should be about 2cm/1in smaller than the diameter of the plate before you stretch it.

Shelves are also an effective and adaptable way of displaying a wide variety of antiques. If you are planning to put several heavy objects on a shelf, make sure it's suitably strong; take advice from your builder if necessary. Don't forget that objects which are openly displayed will need periodic dusting, so it's no good putting them somewhere where it will be impossible for you to reach them from time to time. If you don't want to have to dust so often, consider putting your collection in a glass cabinet or display case.

Small antiques are often more effectively displayed together, rather than dotted around a room. If you have a collection of small silver objects or boxes it might be a good idea to display them on an attractive tray, a dish, or even on a small table.

Antiques of different types look very attractive when displayed together, but always be careful before you place any objects directly on top of old furniture. Silver and metal objects, particularly pieces with feet, can scratch the surface of furniture, so if in doubt place them on a mat to protect the wood.

Finally, once you have displayed your

Opposite Blue and white vases displayed on brackets.
Above A collection of porcelain displayed in an alcove.

collection, don't forget the importance of lighting it effectively, but bear in mind once again that if you stand objects too close to powerful lighting they may be damaged by the heat. Nevertheless, a single spotlight positioned carefully on your display will invariably create a dramatic focal point in any room, whether it's a cluster of plates on a cottage wall, or a group of priceless porcelain figures on the mantelpiece of a stately home.

CARE & RESTORATION

Looking after your antiques correctly is essential if they are to remain in good enough condition for future generations to enjoy as much as you do. Nevertheless, there is a world of difference between caring for an antique correctly and attempting to restore it to mint condition. Almost all antiques reflect their age and you should not expect them to look too perfect.

In general, any restoration work reduces the value of a piece; limited wear and tear will nearly always be preferable and a slightly worn item is usually more valuable than one

Porcelain restoration at West Dean College, Sussex.

which has been over-restored. Nonetheless, if an antique is in danger of deteriorating further because of damage it has sustained, or if its imperfections are impairing your use and enjoyment of it, it may benefit from limited restoration. If this is the case, always consult a specialist restorer. Unskilled restoration can cause irreversible damage to an antique and may greatly reduce its value.

Nearly all antiques, apart from silver, ceramics and glass, should be protected from direct sunlight and heat. Sunlight can cause textiles, carpets, prints and furniture to fade. Direct sources of heat cause many substances, including wood and *papier mâché*, to expand. This may lead to warping and splitting in antique furniture, and can cause cracking or flaking in pieces made from a *papier mâché* core with a painted surface.

Prolonged exposure to cigarette, pipe and tobacco smoke can cause discoloration in many types of antiques which can be tricky to restore. So always keep antiques in a well-ventilated room, and protect them from excessive smoke.

Some general guidelines for caring for the main categories of antiques are listed below; further tips for the proper care of specific types of collectables can be found in Part 3.

FURNITURE

- Excessively dry conditions can cause veneers to lift, and joints to dry out. If you live in a very well heated home it may be worth investing in a humidifier which will help to protect your furniture. However, excessively damp conditions are also detrimental to furniture as they may cause the wood to rot.
- If pieces of veneer break off, don't just throw them away; keep them safely, as it is always preferable to use original veneers in restoration and their use may also reduce the cost of the repairs.
- Avoid silicone polishes and aerosol sprays; instead, use a small amount of good-quality wax polish. Don't polish a piece too often or the surface of the wood may become sticky.
- Never drag antique furniture even a short distance when you want to move it as this causes strain on the legs – pick it up instead. Don't risk picking a piece up by its carrying handle (these are usually more decorative than functional), or by the top if it has a protruding rim; always support the main structure.

CERAMICS AND GLASS

When ceramic pieces are cracked or damaged, the current trend is to leave damage showing, rather than attempt to disguise it completely. Cracked pieces may be stuck together with a suitable glue, but they should not be overpainted. Chips may be filled and coloured to match, but should not be overpainted.

- Pottery, porcelain and glass should occasionally be cleaned by hand with warm soapy water, and should be rinsed off well before they are left to air-dry.
- Decanters should be stored with the stoppers off.
- Do not secure loose lids or stoppers to the main bodies with adhesive tape or adhesive paste as these can easily damage any original gilding and enamel.

Restoration department at Sotheby's, London.

SILVER

Contrary to popular opinion, silver doesn't tarnish especially rapidly unless it's kept in a particularly damp atmosphere. Any proprietary silver polish may be used and a toothbrush may be handy to remove polish from nooks and crannies. Always make sure that you remove all traces of polish, or it can clog up decorated areas. Don't over-polish sliver, or you may erase decoration, and, eventually, wear the metal thin. You can wash silver, by hand, in warm soapy water. Don't put it in the dishwasher as the abrasive powder dulls the surface. Silver gilt doesn't need cleaning with polish; an occasional wash with soapy water should be enough.

- Try not to over-polish Sheffield and electroplate items as you will wear away the thin surface layer of silver.
- Never leave salt in cruets or cellars; salt may get under the glass liner and can cause corrosion spots.

CLOCKS

Most maintenance should be left to a specialist, although wooden cases can be lightly dusted and, occasionally, very lightly waxed. Brass and silvered dials are protected by lacquer and should never be polished or placed in contact with water or detergent.

- Any cleaning and oiling of a clock's movement should be carried out with great care by a specialist.
- Clocks with spring-driven and short pendulums can be carried from one room to another, but should be held upright. For long distance journeys the pendulum must be secured or removed. Longcase clocks should be dismantled before being moved.

CARPETS, RUGS AND TEXTILES

Carpets and rugs should be cleaned by brushing or beating (so long as they are not very frail).

- Placing underlay beneath an antique carpet absorbs wear and protects the pile.
- Sunlight can cause colours to fade and fibres to rot. Framed textiles can be protected by mounting them behind special light-resistant glass.
- Most textiles can be washed with warm soapy water, unless they are very fragile.

PART 3

COLLECTOR'S

COMPENDIUM

ABOVE MEISSEN BLUE AND WHITE SHAPED
RECTANGULAR DISH £4,140

LEFT DOLLS AND TEDDY BEARS ON DISPLAY IN AN
ANTIQUES SHOP

Of all the categories of antiques you can choose to collect, furniture is amongst the most popular. It is one of the largest and most diverse categories, with an enormous number of forms, styles and materials to consider. Furniture is also extremely practical; many pieces offer you the alternative of using them either for their original purpose, or of adapting them to modern-day living. Furniture differs from other types of antiques in that you probably won't want to collect it by the type of object – nobody normally wants a room full of only chests or tables – but you may discover that you have an affinity for a particular wood, period, or style of decoration. Whatever your preference, you need to familiarize yourself with the different decorative styles, methods of construction, and types of materials used, in order to determine whether the piece is "right" (in other words, in its original condition without any major alterations or additions) or "wrong" (which would mean that some major change has been made to it, or it's a fake).

The following pages discuss some of the most common types of furniture you are likely to come across, and give you hints about what to look out for. Once you've read them, visit as many auctions and dealers as possible before you begin to buy. Don't be afraid to examine pieces thoroughly; pull out drawers, get down on the floor and look under table tops, and lift up chairs to look at their legs. Remember there's no better way of learning about the subject than by hands-on experience.

BASICS

No matter what type of furniture you happen to be interested in, there are certain basic considerations which you need to take into account before you decide whether the piece you are examining is genuine, when it was made, and how much it might be worth. Identifying the wood used, the type of construction, the decoration, the quality of workmanship and the overall condition are all crucial in helping you to make up your mind. Information about these fundamental issues, which can be applied to many different types of furniture, will be discussed over the following pages.

WOODS

The first furniture was made from solid wood with carved decoration. However as cabinet-making improved, a new technique of decorating furniture by apply veneers (thin sheets of wood) was developed. This was an economical way of using expensive woods, and allowed the maker to create decorative effects from the different grains and patterns (known as figuring) of the wood. Veneered furniture has a solid body (a carcass) which is made from a different (usually less expensive) wood. This secondary wood, as it is known, is most commonly pine or oak. Listed on the right are examples of the types of woods most frequently used for antique furniture.

AMBOYNA

Richly coloured wood with a tight grain, used during the 18th century and Regency periods, nearly always as a veneer.

BEECH

Brownish-whitish wood used in the solid from the 17th century for the frames of upholstered furniture, because it doesn't split when tacked. Also popular during the 18th and 19th centuries as a base for painted furniture.

CHERRY

Orange-brown wood popular for American Queen Anne and Chippendale furniture. Usually used in the solid.

CHESTNUT

Ranges in tone from light to dark brown,

much used during
the 18th century for
French provincial
furniture made in
the solid.

COROMANDEL

A dark, boldly figured
wood, almost black
in parts with pale
striations, used mainly
as a veneer for refined
furniture of the
Regency period.

EBONY

Dense, heavy, almost
black wood, often used
as a contrasting inlay in
marquetry veneering.

ELM

Light brown-coloured
wood, popular for
Windsor chairs and
provincial English
furniture.

MAHOGANY

Rich golden-
brown or red-brown
coloured wood, it
became popular in
England from c.1730.
There are several
different types of
mahogany, San
Dominguan, Cuban
(also known as Spanish)
and Honduran are the
most common.

OAK

Deep rich chocolate-
brown, or paler golden-
brown coloured
coarse-grained wood
used mainly in Britain
from the Middle Ages
to late 17th century.
Also used as a
secondary wood on
good-quality furniture.

PINE

Soft pale honey-
coloured wood used in
England and America
as a secondary timber,
for drawer linings, and
in the 19th century for
inexpensive furniture
(which was often
painted).

ROSEWOOD

Highly figured dark
red-brown wood with
blackish streaks from
the East Indies and
Brazil. Used for
decoration in the 17th
century, it became
popular during the
Regency and Victorian
periods in Britain for
high-quality furniture.

SATINWOOD

Light yellow-coloured
West Indian wood,
favoured during the
late 18th century.
Usually used in veneers
as it was expensive and
sometimes embellished
with painted
decoration. Painted
satinwood furniture
was also popular in the
Edwardian period.

VIRGINIA WALNUT

Dense, richly coloured
wood resembling
mahogany. Used in the
solid and as a veneer on
English and American
furniture from c.1730.

WALNUT

Nutty or honey-brown
highly figured wood
noted for its excellent
finish. Used in the solid
on English and some
French furniture from
c.1660–c.1690 and as
veneers from c.1690
until c.1735 when it
was supplanted by
mahogany. Walnut was
also popular in America
and the Victorian era.

YEW

Red-brown or honey-
coloured hardwood
used both in veneers or
in the solid on the best
English provincial
furniture of the 17th
and 18th centuries.

COLOUR AND PATINA

A rich mellow colour
is one of the most
important features of
any piece of furniture.
The *patina* is the glow
the wood develops over
the years from an
accumulation of wax
polish and dirt.

- Most furniture is not
  the same colour all
  over – grooves and
  carving will look
  darker, surfaces
  exposed to sunlight
  may be lighter.
- Deep *patina* is less
  favoured by the
  European market,
  where furniture
  is often stripped
  and repolished.

PROPORTIONS

The proportions are
fundamental in
assessing the quality of
a piece, and deciding
whether it's "right".

- A piece which looks
  too heavy on top, or
  has legs which are
  too big or small may
  well be a "marriage"
  (see p41).
- Small pieces are
  often more desirable.

CONSTRUCTION

Early furniture was made using mortice-and-tenon joints held by pegs or dowels (below) instead of glue or screws. This method was used until the late 17th century. Pegs were handmade and stand slightly proud of the surface.

- Later machine-made pegs are perfectly symmetrical and are either flush with the surface or slightly recessed.

- From the early 18th century joints were dovetailed and glued (above).
- Until the end of the 18th century, when the circular saw was introduced, all wood was sawed by hand and has straight saw marks. After c.1800 circular marks may be visible on the surface of unfinished wood.

SCREWS

The earlier the screw the cruder it will be.
- The groove on old screws tends to be off-centre and the top irregular (top).
- The thread is also irregular and open and, unlike modern screws (above), runs the entire length of the shank.

DRAWERS

- Dovetails are the triangular joints which slot together on the corners of drawers. They became progressively finer (see p43) and can help with dating.
- Drawers had channels in their sides and, until the 18th century, ran on runners set into the carcass.
- Some drawers ran on the dust boards and had no runners.
- From the Queen Anne period the runners were placed under the drawer at the sides and ran on bearers placed on the inside of the carcass.

HANDLES

- Handles can provide a useful clue to dating, because styles changed from period to period (see p42).
- It's common to find pieces with replaced handles; this isn't serious but it's preferable to have handles in keeping with the rest of the piece.
- From c.1690 handles were secured by pommels and nuts.

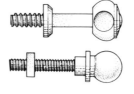

- Antique pommels were hand-cast in a single piece of brass (top). The thread goes only halfway up the shank, and the remainder of the shank is square-shaped. Modern pommels (above) are made from brass heads with steel shanks and the thread runs the whole length of the shank.
- The nuts used to attach handles in the 18th century were circular and slightly irregular. Modern nuts are regular and hexagonal.

FEET

Feet can give a useful guide to dating (see p42); however, centuries of standing on damp floors often causes feet to rot and may therefore have been replaced.
- Compare the wood of the feet with that of the rest of the body to decide whether or not they're original.

LOCKS

- Early locks are usually of wrought iron held in place with iron nails. From the 18th century locks were steel or brass and secured with steel screws.
- Locks are often replaced; this isn't serious although it's better to have original ones.

CARVING

Oak was relatively difficult to carve but as walnut and mahogany became popular carving became finer and more intricate.
- Original carved decoration adds to the desirability of a piece.

- Some pieces were adorned with later carving; these are far less desirable than those with original decoration.

VENEERING

The quality of veneering has an important bearing on price.

- Many pieces have *quarter-veneered* tops, where four pieces of wood create a pattern.
- *Banding*, strips of veneers laid around the edges of drawers, was also popular. Depending on the way in which the grain of the wood runs, banding is referred to as *straight banding, cross-banding, feather* or *herringbone banding*.

INLAY AND MARQUETRY

A pattern made from veneers of different

coloured woods (see p44). Inlaying was popular on English and Continental furniture from the 17th century and can add greatly to the value of a piece. Marquetry is the technique of cutting shapes in a veneer and first became popular in England in the late 17th century.

GILDING

The additionof gold leaf as decoration on a carved softwood frame (usually beech) has four stages. The wood is sealed and made perfectly smooth with a chalky layer of gesso; a layer of bol-coloured red or yellow is applied to give depth and richness to the gilding; the gold leaf is applied with a brush and glued in place; finally, the desired shine is created by burnishing the surface with an agate.

CONDITION

Furniture in original pristine condition commands the highest prices and is always extremely scarce.

- Don't dismiss pieces with blemishes – as long as the wood itself has not been damaged; surface spots can often be treated by a good restorer. The table

(below left) may look rather scruffy but the wood itself is undamaged and could easily be repolished.

WOODWORM

Small round holes in old furniture are a common sight and show that the piece has at some stage been attacked by woodworm.

- These need not put you off, provided the infestation hasn't structurally weakened the piece.
- Active woodworm can be detected by pale-coloured powder in the worm holes, or on adjacent surfaces, and should be treated with a proprietary product as soon as possible.
- Check all your pieces periodically for signs of infestation.

MARRIAGES

A piece of furniture made up from separate items which did not originally belong together is termed a "marriage".

- The married parts may be of a similar period or one part may be later, or even modern.
- Marriages are nearly always much less

desirable than pieces in their original condition.

- Examine furniture in the way described on p38 to make sure it isn't a marriage.

ALTERATIONS

Furniture which has been altered is usually less desirable than that in its original condition. Among the most common alterations are large pieces which have been reduced in size. Freshly cut surfaces, repositioned handles, and plugged holes are signs of alteration.

FAKES

A piece of furniture can be described as fake if it deliberately makes you think it's older than it really is. Fakes made from new timber are usually easy to spot as the wood doesn't have the patina of age you would expect. Some fakes are made from old wood and these can be more tricky to identify. Beware of any piece being sold as 18th century or earlier if it has circular saw marks (see p40). These mean the wood was cut after c.1800 when circular saws were first used. Specific types of fake are dealt with in Part 3.

CHESTS

Chests of drawers are among the most indispensable pieces of furniture for storage and, not surprisingly, have been made in huge numbers over the centuries. They are still among the most easily available and inexpensive pieces of antique furniture – although of course there are rare and expensive ones as well.

A chest has many of the elements found in other types of furniture – drawers, feet, handles and so on – and if you're keen to learn how to date and authenticate any type of antique furniture, examining a chest carefully can teach you a great deal.

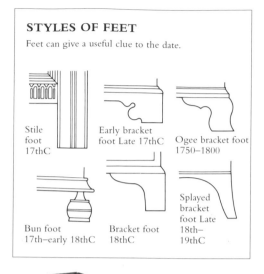

STYLES OF FEET

Feet can give a useful clue to the date.

Stile foot 17thC

Early bracket foot Late 17thC

Ogee bracket foot 1750–1800

Bun foot 17th–early 18thC

Bracket foot 18thC

Splayed bracket foot Late 18th–19thC

HANDLE STYLES

Late 17th–early 18thC

Early 18thC

2nd quarter 18thC

2nd half 18thC

Late 18thC–early 19thC

◀ **WALNUT CHESTS**
Size has an important bearing on the price of all chests. Although this walnut-veneered 18th century chest is in a sorry state, it's desirably small (77cm/2ft 6in wide) and so is still worth £2,000–4,000.

◀ **MAHOGANY CHESTS**
Mahogany chests, such as this (made *c.*1765), are more common than walnut ones and so are usually less expensive. This chest is of exceptionally high quality, but even so need not cost much more than the battered walnut one above. £2,000–4,000.

WHY DO DEALERS LOOK IN DRAWERS?

When looking at a chest (or any piece with drawers) always pull each one out and examine it carefully. Marks in the wood, tiny holes and joints all have things to tell us. Look for marks on the dustboards inside – if the chest is original the marks of the runners should correspond with marks on the bottom of the drawer. From c.1790 drawers were strengthened by baseboards running from side to side with a central rib.

CONSTRUCTION

Examine the dovetails – they can tell you when the drawer was made. The earliest drawers have three coarse dovetails; later drawers usually have four or five finer ones. Don't just look at one drawer – check them all to make sure that they're all made and worn in the same way.

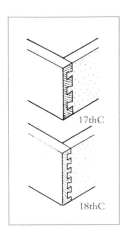

17thC

18thC

This mahogany chest was made c.1790; the bow-fronted style remained popular throughout much of the 19th century. £500–3,500

HANDLES

Check drawers inside and out for marks, such as holes or the outline of an old handle shape, where different handles might once have been. However, don't be put off if the handles have been replaced – it's very common. and should not decrease desirability.

UNDERSIDES

Don't expect chests to be neatly finished all the way round. They were made to stand against a wall and their backs and undersides are usually made from rough unpolished boards.

FEET

The feet are most prone to wear and are often replaced, so check the colour and grain of each one. These feet are original and look appropriately battered.

DRESSERS, CABINETS & CREDENZAS

In the minds of most collectors antique dressers epitomize a particularly "country" style and an image of rustic charm. They give instant atmosphere to a room and can look equally impressive standing in a dining room, kitchen or hall – or wherever else you might care to put them. Dressers vary greatly in price according to the style you are looking for; those made from simple pine during the 19th century, or later, are most likely to be affordable; early ones, especially those made of oak, are usually very much more expensive.

In contrast to dressers, cabinets are considered to be among the most refined – and therefore valuable – pieces of antique furniture available. They were made in the 17th and 18th centuries and were specifically designed to store precious curiosities, and became status symbols reflecting the wealth and taste of their owner. Cabinets can create a dramatic focal point in any room – but unless you are extremely lucky, you will probably have to dig deep in your pocket to be able to afford an early one.

If your budget means that you seek a more affordable elegance look out for 19th century credenzas. Like cabinets, credenzas were made to display collections of valuables, and they are often highly ornate and decorative. Unlike most early cabinets, however, some are still available at relatively inexpensive prices.

▼ **CABINETS**

Legs on cabinets have often been replaced. Even though the stand of this *c.*1690 oyster laburnum marquetry cabinet is actually a later replacement (it has a harsh glossy finish quite different from the mellow sheen of the rest of the piece), the cabinet is still very valuable and worth around £7,000–9,000.

MARQUETRY

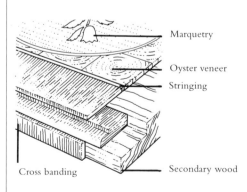

Marquetry

Oyster veneer

Stringing

Cross banding

Secondary wood

Marquetry, like that seen on the 17th century cabinet above, always adds to value. Terms used to describe the different techniques are:

- **Oyster veneering:** slices cut across branches to make patterns like an oyster shell.
- **Cross-banding:** border with a grain at right angles to the main veneer.
- **Parquetry:** geometric pattern of small pieces of veneer.
- **Stringing:** narrow line of inlaid wood.

WHAT TO LOOK FOR

Early (pre-*c.*1800) dressers have some recognisable features:
- simple joined construction
- rather crudly made drawers
- at least three drawers across base – if there are two it may have been reduced in size.

DRESSERS

Beware of dressers where the base and rack have been "married" and did not originally belong together. Not all dressers had racks so watch for anything out of place. Compare the colour and patina of wood on both parts – here the colour of rack and base are similar, showing that they belong together. Look for the outline of the rack on the base, such as you can see here. £3,000–5,000.

▶ **CREDENZAS**

Some credenzas, especially ebonized examples, can still be bought for under £2,000 – a bargain considering their usual good quality, especially when you compare them with the cost of earlier similarly elaborate pieces. This one, however, is worth around £2,500–3,500 and has many desirable features:
- walnut veneers
- original glass
- gilt mounts
- attractive inlay.

CHAIRS

Chairs are among the most essential pieces of furniture, and not surprisingly the finest antique ones – usually those made in the 18th century or earlier – can be very valuable. Prices for dining chairs are not only affected by quality and age, but also by the number of chairs in the set – the larger the set the more expensive each chair becomes. But if you choose a simple pattern you may be able to find odd numbers of chairs and build up a set piecemeal.

The first chairs were simply constructed like stools, with a plank of wood at the back which sometimes had carved decoration. During the second half of the 17th century walnut replaced oak as the favourite wood and chairs were often elaborately carved with scrolls on stretchers and legs.

Mahogany chairs became popular during the 18th century, and chair styles reflected designs published by leading designers such as Chippendale, Hepplewhite and Sheraton. Pattern books of their designs were circulated nationwide to many local cabinet-makers, who reproduced the designs, often in much simplified form. Nowadays, when a chair is described as "Chippendale", "Hepplewhite" or "Sheraton" it usually means it is based on one of their patterns rather than made by the cabinet-maker himself.

DATING CHAIRS

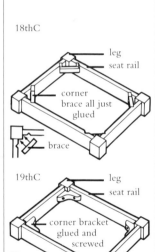

18thC

leg
seat rail
corner brace all just glued
brace

19thC

leg
seat rail
corner bracket glued and screwed
corner bracket

Before the 19th century, chair seat frames were strengthened with glued corner braces. After c.1840 shaped and screwed triangular brackets were used.

▼ EARLY OAK CHAIRS

Carving can help identify a chair's origins. This one dates from c.1640 and is carved with the dragon crest and scrolled arms typical of the Gloucestershire region. £1,500–5,000.

▲ WALNUT CHAIRS

This c. 1720 walnut chair has the cabriole legs and drop-in seat characteristic of chairs of the period. However, high-quality chairs of this date would not normally have had stretchers so this one was probably made by a provincial maker rather than a major name. £300+

THOMAS CHIPPENDALE

Many of Thomas Chippendale's chair designs featured pierced splats carved with scrolling foliage and incorporating Gothic elements, just as seen on this *c.*1765 chair. Ribbons and chinoiserie details were also popular motifs which he used freely. £750+

WHAT TO LOOK FOR

- Examine each chair carefully for signs of genuine wear and the patina of age – nearly all types have been reproduced.
- If the colour of one part looks very different it may be replaced.
- Thick brown varnish often indicates a chair trying to look older than it is.

▼ REGENCY CHAIRS

This *c.*1800 painted chair, with gilded decoration, slender arms and ebonized and tapered front legs is typical of the early Regency period. Later chairs were more heavily proportioned. £500–2,000

▼ BALLOON-BACKED CHAIRS

The value of this *c.*1860 Victorian walnut balloon-back chair is increased by its fine proportions and desirable needlework seat. £300–400

▲ WINDSOR CHAIRS

Windsors are made from country woods such as elm, oak, ash and yew and usually date from after *c.*1700. Yew Windsors, like this one, made *c.*1810, are the most sought-after. The curved crinoline stretcher between the legs is unusual at this date. £500+

CHAIR STYLES

The changing styles of chair backs, legs and feet can help collectors to date chairs. The illustrations show a selection of the more commonly seen designs. However, as most of these were repeated in later periods, the style of a chair must be seen only as a guide to its age, not as proof of its authenticity.

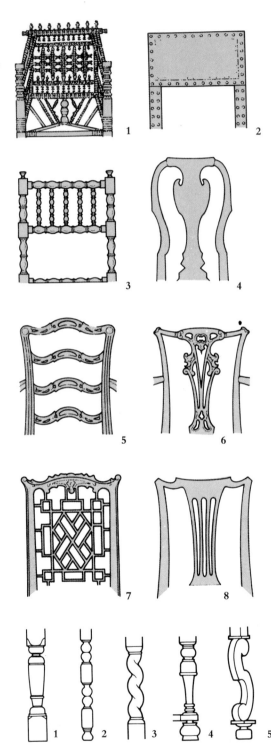

CHAIR BACKS

1 Early 16thC bobbin frame
2 Cromwellian padded
3 Late 17thC bobbin turned
4 Early 18thC Queen Anne hoop-back with urn-shaped splat
5 Ladder-back with horizontal pierced splats, *c.*1760
6 Chippendale-style with carved splat *c.*1760
7 "Chinese" Chippendale chair *c.*1760
8 Plain mahogany Chippendale-style chair *c.*1760
9 Late 18thC Hepplewhite-style shield back
10 Late 18thC Gothic-style chair
11 Late 18thC lyre-back
12 Early 19thC country-style ladder back
13 Late 18thC hoop-back with wheatsheaf
14 Sheraton-style arm chair *c.*1790
15 Early 19thC Sheraton-style square framed
16 Late 18thC Gothic Windsor
17 Early 19thC spindle-back
18 Early 19thC plain Windsor

19 Regency with key pattern *c.* 1820
20 Regency rope twist *c.*1820
21 Early Victorian *c.*1940
22 Gothic square-backed *c.*1830
23 Victorian carved balloon-back *c.*1850
24 Mid-19thC Victorian Carolean

LEGS AND FEET

1 16thC baluster
2 Late 17thC bobbin turned
3 Second half 17thC barley-twist
4 Inverted cup baluster *c.*1675–1700
5 Late 17thC double scroll
6 Early 18thC cabriole
7 Early 18thC carved cabriole
8 18thC shell-carved cabriole
9 Early Georgian carved cabriole
10 Mid-18thC cabriole with claw-and-ball foot
11 Chamfered *c.*1750–80
12 Mid-18thC blind fretted
13 Late 18thC turned
14 Early 19thC sabre
15 Victorian Carolean *c.*1845
16 Mid-19thC reeded

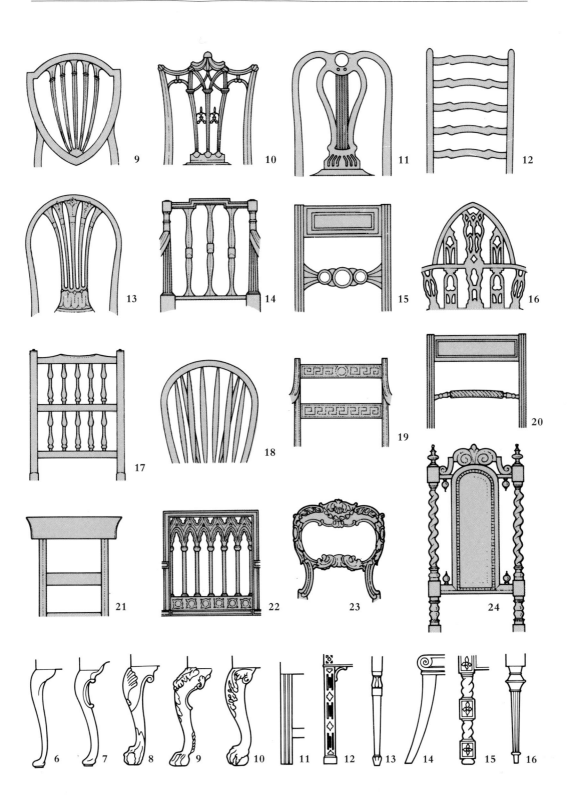

UPHOLSTERED CHAIRS & SOFAS

No home would be complete without comfy sofas and chairs, and antique upholstered furniture can sometimes be less expensive than modern counterparts – and surprisingly comfortable as well.

Among the most popular types of chairs are winged armchairs with simple cabriole legs and side panels to keep out chilly draughts.

These were first made in the early 18th century and the design has remained virtually unchanged to this day. The wooden frame is the most important part of antique chairs and sofas, so never buy a chair with a severely damaged frame. Don't worry too much about the condition of upholstery – as this can usually be restored.

WING ARM CHAIRS

◄ SIGNS OF AGE
The marks left by the original upholstery nails are still clearly visible on the side of the chair and are a good indication that it is an original and not a more recent reproduction.

▲ BEFORE
Although this arm chair (shown on the right after it had been re-upholstered) looks terribly tatty, being able to see it like this is a bonus – you can make sure the wood is original and hasn't split or been weakened by woodworm.

● If the chair is recently re-covered, ask if there are photos of the frame.

▶ AFTER
It's very rare to find a chair with its original covering but provided the fabric is in a style appropriate to the chair the re-upholstering doesn't greatly affect value – this 18th century chair is covered in a suitable silk damask. £5,000+

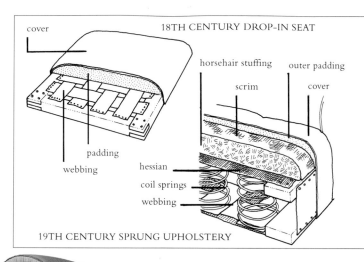

18TH CENTURY DROP-IN SEAT

cover

horsehair stuffing   outer padding

scrim   cover

padding

webbing   hessian

coil springs

webbing

19TH CENTURY SPRUNG UPHOLSTERY

WHAT'S INSIDE A CHAIR?

Before *c*.1830 the upholstery on chairs was made from thin layers of horsehair and padding supported by webbing covered with fabric. Upholstery using coiled metal springs covered with padding and webbing was made from *c*.1830.

▲ REGENCY CHAISES LONGUES
The outward curving "sabre" legs, dark painted wood, and "anthemion" flower decorations are clear signs that this elegant chaise longue dates from the Regency period (*c*.1815). Although not very comfortable, chaises longues have become enormously popular recently; this one could fetch £5,000 or more.

◀ BUTTON-BACKS
Before buying a Victorian button-back, turn it upside down and look for a manufacturer's mark or label; these can add greatly to value – Howard & Sons' labels are especially desirable – they made what is considered the "Rolls-Royce" of chairs! This particular armchair is worth over £3,000, but it is possible to find other examples from around £500+.

DINING TABLES

PEDESTAL TABLES

Elegant pedestal tables are so practical and popular that they have been made continuously from the 18th century to the present day. Value depends largely on age and number of pedestals. A 19th century one such as this might cost from £3,000 upwards, a modern version £300–500.

BEFORE YOU BUY IT...

fit any extra leaves in the table to check that they haven't warped.

SIGNS OF AGE

- solid mahogany tops (usually without cross-banding or inlay)
- "reeded" edge to tops
- brass casters – plain or cast as lion's paws.

There are many different types of dining table to choose from, depending on what size you require – and how much you want to spend. Remember to look at the grain of the wood on the top – an attractively grained top is a definite plus but will increase the price. If you're on a limited budget don't dismiss tables which have marked tops – so long as the wood has not been damaged it can probably be restored to its former glory. Don't forget to sit down at the table to make sure it feels a comfortable height and the legs don't get in the way of yours.

WHAT TO LOOK FOR

- Signs of wear on the legs and top – scratches and marks are a sign of genuine age and to be expected.
- Legs of more or less the same colour – if one is noticeably different it might be a later replacement.
- Flaps which match the rest of the table reasonably well – those used only occasionally may not have faded as much as the rest of the table but their figuring should be similar.

◀ **REFECTORY
TABLES**
These are among the
earliest dining tables;
most date from the
17th–18th centuries,
but there are also fakes
around – many made
from old floorboards.
Look for circular saw
marks – these show the
table is not as old as it
seems and has been
tampered with since
the 19th century. This
one dates from *c*.1620
and is worth over
£10,000.

▶ **DROP LEAF
TABLES**
Drop leafs with simple
pad feet like this are
among the most
affordable types of 18th
century tables; this one
would cost around
£500+.

▲ **D-ENDED TABLES**
Adaptable D-ended
tables come in several
sections; the ends can
be used as side tables.
£1,500–4,000

▶ **GATELEG
TABLES**
Hinged "gates" pull
out to hold up the
flaps on these
17th/18th century
tables – hence their
name. The most
expensive ones seat
six or more. £1,000+

BEWARE
Some tops are
"married" (see p41)
to different bases:
look carefully
under the top –
marks which could
have been made by
different supports
should make you
suspicious.

SMALLER TABLES

Most of the myriad types of small table date from the 18th century or later. Before this, side tables were mainly general purpose and often rectangular in shape. As fashionable society became increasingly sophisticated, furniture became more varied and elegant and a wide range of small tables designed for specific purposes, such as tea-drinking, card playing or sewing, were made; nowadays these can be just as useful for putting the telephone on as for their original function. Small tables fit easily into most modern homes so they have remained very sought after. Pairs are always especially desirable.

▶ TRIPOD TABLES
Carving is easily damaged and can be expensive to restore. The value of this 18th century tilt-top table is reduced because the "pie-crust" rim has been chipped. £2,500

▲ CARD TABLES
The projecting circular corners of this 18th century table are stands for candles needed to illuminate cards and chips during play. £2,000+

◀ WORK TABLES
Work tables, such as this one made c.1810 from satinwood, have drawers and a pull out bag to hold sewing materials. £2,500+

▲ SOFA TABLES
The best sofa tables have two end-supports connected by a stretcher, as in this example. Tables with a central pedestal base are less valuable. £1,500+

▲ PAINTED SATINWOOD
You can distinguish Georgian painted satinwood tables – such as this pier table made *c.*1775 – from their early 20th century counterparts by:
● the pale mellow colour of the wood
● the less colourful painted decoration. Later tables are less valuable. Because of its age this one is worth about £8,000 but it would only cost about £1,500–2,000 if it was 20th century.

TABLE STYLES

Type	First made	Price and typical wood	Description
Card & Games	*c.*1700	£800+ mahogany, walnut, satinwood	Usually rectangular or *demi-lune* with folding top, baize-covered inside, specifically made for cards and other games
Console	*c.*1720	£1,000+ giltwood	Rectangular, sometimes with serpentine front and only two front legs or carved base: made to stand against the wall
Drum	*c.*1800	£1,000+ mahogany	Circular with frieze containing drawers; central pedestal support
Pembroke	*c.*1750	£500+ mahogany, satinwood	Rectangular, serpentine or oval, with curved corners, drop flaps and drawers
Quartetto	*c.*1790	£1,000+ mahogany, rosewood, walnut	Set of tables which reduce in size to fit under each other
Sofa	*c.*1790	£800+ mahogany, rosewood, satinwood	Elongated rectangle with drop flaps and drawers
Tripod	*c.*1700	£300+ mahogany	Round tilt-top, tripod base usually made from solid wood

SIDEBOARDS & DINING ACCESSORIES

Even after you have chosen your table and chairs, no matter what your preferred style, there's a wealth of other antique accessories available for the dining room.

Large pieces, such as serving tables and sideboards, became extremely elegant and sophisticated during the 18th century, and many are now very expensive. Much more reasonably priced are the wealth of 19th century sideboards available; and surprisingly the largest examples are often also the most affordable.

You can also find an extraordinary array of smaller dining room accessories, such as wine coolers, urns, knife boxes, cellarets and dumb waiters. Most were originally made with a very specific function in mind but can nevertheless be surprisingly versatile. These days wine coolers are more often used as containers for flowers than for wine, but they are still highly collectable.

▲ URNS
You might think that these attractive urns are purely decorative; in fact they open up and some were fitted out to hold knives, while others have spouts for iced drinking water. Pairs of Georgian urns are especially desirable. These ones were made *c*.1775 and would cost around £5,000–7,000.

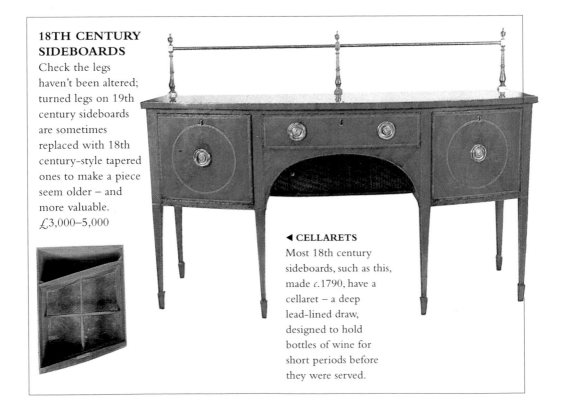

18TH CENTURY SIDEBOARDS
Check the legs haven't been altered; turned legs on 19th century sideboards are sometimes replaced with 18th century-style tapered ones to make a piece seem older – and more valuable.
£3,000–5,000

◀ CELLARETS
Most 18th century sideboards, such as this, made *c*.1790, have a cellaret – a deep lead-lined draw, designed to hold bottles of wine for short periods before they were served.

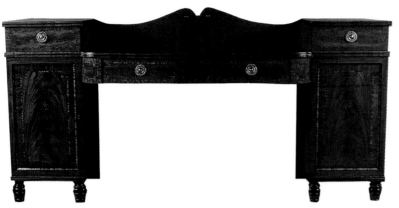

◀ LATER SIDEBOARDS
Provided you have the room, you can still find some larger 19th century sideboards in reasonable condition for £1,000–1,500; this one dates from *c.*1815, and would be worth £2,500–3,500.

HOW OLD IS IT?
This Gothic Chippendale-style side table might look 18th century but in fact was made *c.*1910. One telltale sign is the dull flat sheen of the wood – an older piece would have a mellow glowing patina. £1,500–3,000

CELLARET OR WINE COOLER?
Wine coolers were used for cooling bottles in ice before their contents were drunk. They rarely have lids and may have a plug in the base. Lidded containers for storing wine, such as this, are properly described as cellarets, but the terms overlap. £1,500+

▶ Wine coolers and cellarets can usually be dated from their style.

*c.*1760

*c.*1790

*c.*1770

*c.*1815

DESKS & BUREAUX

There are many different types of "writing furniture", but perhaps the best known is the bureau, basically a desk with a hinged flat that folds up when not in use. Made in quantity from the 18th century, bureaux are generally oak, walnut or mahogany, sometimes lavishly decorated with lacquer or marquetry. They were often combined with bookcases and cabinets to become bureau bookcases or bureau cabinets. Like ordinary cabinets, these were as much to display the wealth of their owner as for any practical purpose. Many bureaux have a strong architectural feel and were designed to co-ordinate with the architecture of the room in which they stood. Other forms of writing furniture included writing tables, kneehole desks and the curiously shaped davenport.

▼ 18TH CENTURY BUREAUX

This early 18th century bureau has many typical features which you should look for:

- small size – those wider than 107cm (42in) are less desirable
- attractive walnut veneers
- bun feet, although most are replacements.

Circular saw marks in the baseboard (below) show that a bureau originally had bracket feet (even if it now has bun feet).
£3,000–6,000

LACQUER & JAPANNING

Chinese and Japanese lacquer became popular in the 17th century, and soon English cabinet-makers began to produce their own "Oriental"-style lacquer called japanning. Black was the most common colour; red, as on this desk, is much rarer.

▲ KNEEHOLE DESKS

Kneehole desks are sometimes converted from chests of drawers, so check that the drawers look complete and that veneers match. Avoid a desk with drawers on one side only – it's probably a converted washstand!

- Most desks are made from walnut, mahogany, or pine. The wood of this one is covered with red japanning which means that it is worth. £10,000+

DATING
Pediments can help with dating

Double dome top
1690–1720

Broken pediment
1730–1800

American
bonnet top
1730–1760

Swan-neck
pediment
1760–1810

Regency top
1800–1830

Moulded dentil
1780–1810

▼ DAVENPORTS
There are two main
types of davenport.
Early ones were quite
plain and had an upper
section which pulled
forward to provide the
writing surface. By
c.1840 many had the
desirable "piano-rise'
top (which opens like a
piano) and a recess
case, like the one
shown here. Expect to
pay more for good-
quality woods, like
satinwood, rosewood,
or the burr walnut of
this piece which is
worth about
£3,000–4,500.

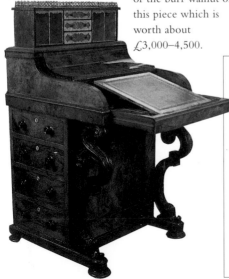

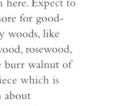

WHAT TO LOOK FOR
- Bureau bookcases and
  secretaire bookcases
- Bookcases should be
  slightly smaller than
  their base, but made
  of matching wood.
- **Beware** of bases and
  tops which are flush
  sided – they could be a
  marriage or cut-down
  library bookcase.

**▲ SECRETAIRE
BOOKCASES**
The secretaire
bookcase first became
popular in the late 18th
century. When the deep
top drawer is open the
front "drops" to form
the writing surface. The
fine-quality interior of
this piece will be
reflected in the price –
about £15,000 – a
lesser one might be as
little as £1,500.

MISCELLANEOUS FURNITURE

Antique furniture is not confined solely to the main types covered on the previous pages. There is also an extensive array of other interesting and attractive pieces, which, although they do not fall into any particular category, are nonetheless extremely popular with antiques collectors.

▶ MIRRORS

Don't confuse carved giltwood mirrors, such as this one, made *c.*1750, with later gilded composition ones. If you can see a cement-like substance over a wire frame on any undecorated areas, rather than wood, it is a composition mirror – and it will therefore be worth only a fraction of this giltwood mirror's £3,000+ price.

▲ OAK COFFERS

You can still find plain 17th and 18th century coffers for a few hundred pounds. Original carving, as seen here, adds to value; but be suspicious of any carving that seems unusually regular and stiff – it could well have been added in the 19th century.
£1,000–3,000

◀ FIRE SCREENS

Because many 17th and 18th century ladies' cosmetics were made with wax, fire screens, such as this short pole screen with a tapestry panel, were developed. They provided essential protection from the roaring fires, to stop their make-up melting and dripping down their faces! £500+

◀ BEDS
Nothing can give a more sumptuous look to a bedroom than an antique bed, but before you buy one remember they are often smaller than modern beds so you may need to have a mattress specially made. Nearly all four-poster (tester) beds have been changed in some way. Many are composites from different periods. This one has panels dating from *c.*1600 combined with later additions. £5,000

▼ STOOLS
Although the stool is the simplest type of seat furniture, don't expect to find them all at rock-bottom prices – they can be surprisingly valuable.

This pair of French mid-18th century X-frame stools would be worth over £3,000 – but you could well find a Victorian or Edwardian stool for much less.

▲ COMMODES
Originally dubbed "night tables" during the prudish Victorian era, cupboards for chamberpots were renamed "commodes" – the name has stayed the same ever since. £850–2,500

Ceramics can be broadly divided into two main groups: pottery, which is opaque when held to the light, and porcelain, which is translucent. Within these two categories there is a huge range of different types of wares which have evolved over the centuries as new manufacturing techniques were developed.

If you're just beginning your collection the multitude of English pottery wares produced during the 19th century could be an ideal starting point. During this period factories in the Staffordshire area produced an enormous number and variety of inexpensive household and decorative objects. At the time these pieces cost a few shillings or less and they are still abundantly available and, although collectable, they have remained relatively inexpensive.

Porcelain has long been highly prized by collectors and as a result tends to be more expensive than pottery. The field is divided into two main groups: hard-paste porcelain and soft-paste porcelain. Many pieces have manufacturer's marks of some type. These can provide useful information about both origin and date, but they are no guarantee of authenticity. Many factories copied other's marks to make their products more desirable and in China pieces were often marked with earlier dates to show respect for earlier potters.

Value is usually a matter of size, age, rarity, decorative appeal and, above all, condition. European 18th century porcelain tends to be very highly priced but you can often buy damaged pieces for a fraction of the cost of those in perfect condition.

BASICS

When you first examine a piece of pottery or porcelain, having a basic understanding of the materials or techniques used in its manufacture can help you identify its origin, date and how much it might be worth. The three main factors to assess are:

- Material
- Glaze
- Decoration

MATERIALS
Pottery
This has a relatively coarse texture, compared with porcelain, and is usually opaque if held to the light; the two main types are earthenware and non-porous stoneware.

Earthenware
Clay fired at a temperature of less than 2200°F (1200°C) is classified as earthenware. The body is porous, and may be of a white, buff, brown, red or grey colour, depending on the colour of the clay and on the iron content.

Stoneware
This is made from clay which can withstand firing at a temperature up to 2250°F (1400°C). The high firing temperature makes the clay fuse into a non-porous body which does not absorb liquids, and may be semi-translucent. Bodies vary in colour.

Porcelain
If the material is slightly translucent the chances are it's porcelain; now you must decide which type – hard-paste or soft-paste. If the body looks smooth, like icing sugar, it's probably hard-paste, if it looks granular, like sand, it's more likely to be soft-paste.

Hard-paste porcelain

A hard-paste porcelain Meissen quatrefoil dish £4,000–5,000

All Chinese and much Continental porcelain is hard-paste, and made from kaolin (china clay) and petuntse (china stone). First the object is fired, then dipped in glaze, then refined. The china stone bonds the particles of clay together and gives translucency. The firing takes place at a very high temperature and so the finished object appears to have the consistency of glass.

The first hard-paste porcelain was made in China in the 9th century AD. In Europe the Meissen factory began producing porcelain in the early 18th century, and before long, factories throughout Europe began making hard-paste porcelain.

Soft-paste porcelain

A Chelsea soft-paste porcelain group depicting Winter and Spring £4,000–5,000

As the name suggests, soft-paste porcelain is more vulnerable to scratching than hard-paste. There are several types of soft-paste porcelain, each using fine clay combined with different ingredients to give translucency.

Soft-paste can often be identified because the glaze sits on the surface, feeling warmer and softer to the touch and looking less glittering in appearance than hard-paste. Chips in soft-paste look floury, like fine pastry; chips in hard-paste porcelain look glassy.

Soft-paste porcelain was first produced in Italy during the 16th century. Later factories using soft-paste include St Cloud, Chantilly, Vincennes, Sèvres, Capodimonte and Chelsea.

Bone china

This is a type of English porcelain first made *c*.1794 using a large proportion of bone ash added to hard-paste ingredients. This body was used by prominent English factories such as Spode, Flight & Barr, Derby, Rockingham, Coalport and Minton.

GLAZES

Glazes are used to make a porous body watertight and also to decorate a piece. They can be translucent, opaque, or coloured. Hard-paste porcelain was given a feldspar glaze, which fused with the body when fired. On soft-paste porcelain the glaze tends to pool in the crevices.

A variety of different glazes were used on pottery and porcelain and each type has its own distinctive characteristics; the main ones are:

A Dutch delftware tin glaze tortoise £2,000–2,500

Lead glaze

A glaze used on most soft-paste porcelain, and on earthenwares such as creamware.

Tin glaze

A glaze to which tin oxide has been added to give an opaque white finish.

Salt glaze

A glassy looking glaze formed by throwing common salt into the kiln during the firing when the temperature reaches about 1800°F (1000°C).

DECORATIVE TECHNIQUES

Decoration can be added before or after glazing. Underglaze decoration means the colours have been added before glazing.

Underglaze blue

Blue pigment, known as cobalt blue, was used on Chinese blue and white porcelain, European delftware, and soft-paste porcelain.

Overglaze enamels

Overglaze enamels were made by adding metallic oxide to molten glass and reducing the cooled mixture, which, when combined with an oily medium, could be painted over the glaze and fused to it by firing. The range of colours was larger than with underglaze colours.

MARKS

Marks are found on the bases of many objects. The most common examples are the factory marks; the Worcester crescent or Meissen's crossed swords. The style of these marks changes periodically and can therefore help with dating. Other marks which appear refer to the individuals involved in the manufacturing. Maker's initials are fairly common, but some designers, decorators modellers and even gilders signed pieces.

● Many marks were copied or faked so marks should not be taken as a guarantee of authenticity.

CHINESE POTTERY & PORCELAIN

Mention Chinese ceramics and many people immediately think of priceless Ming and assume that this collecting area is definitely beyond their reach. In fact, because fine pottery and porcelain have been produced in China for longer than anywhere else in the world, it's not hard to find pieces that are both decorative and inexpensive – although there are of course some extremely highly priced objects as well.

The Chinese discovered the art of making porcelain in the Tang Dynasty, AD618–906. When Dutch traders began importing Chinese porcelain to Europe in the 17th century (the late Ming period) no European maker had yet been able to produce such fine -quality wares and there was a huge demand for Chinese porcelain – as well as a scramble to find out how it was made (see p62). Nearly all porcelain was blue and white until *c.*1700, when more varied colour schemes such as *famille rose* and *famille verte* were introduced. The many objects made for the European market, often using Western shapes but decorated with traditional Chinese designs, are known collectively as "export wares".

LATER CHINESE DYNASTIES

Wei	386–557	Sung	960–1280
Sui	589–617	Chin	1115–1260
Tang	618–906	Yuan	1280–1368
5 Dyn-		Ming	1368–1644
asties	907–960	Qing	1644–1916
Liao	907–1125		

MING
Value depends on quality and condition. Provincial export pieces of lesser quality, or slightly chipped or cracked wares, can be surprisingly affordable. This bowl would be worth over £100,000 but you can find pieces from about £100.

BEWARE
Don't rely on dynasty reign marks alone for dating Chinese porcelain – as many as 80% are retrospective, and were simply used to show respect for earlier classical wares.

MING OR QING?
Ming patterns were often repeated during the Qing period; Ming pieces can be identified by:
- thick bluish glaze, suffused with bubbles
- tendency to reddish oxidization
- knife marks on the tallish foot-rim.

▲ BLUE AND WHITE

Chinese blue and white was made by painting the blue decoration onto the porcelain base, before glazing – a technique known as "underglaze blue". Later wares, such as these

Qing export vases (worth £8,000–10,000) can be identified by:

- complicated designs
- harder, more evenly applied blue
- thinner glaze.

▲ FAMILLE VERTE

Famille verte ("green family") porcelain is dominated by a brilliant green colour, overglaze blue and raised enamelling. It was used to decorate export wares from the Kangxi period (1662–1722). £5,000–6,000

▲ FAMILLE ROSE

Wares decorated with opaque pink enamel are termed famille rose ("pink family") and appeared c.1718. The style was often copied in the 19th century particularly by the French maker Samson: crackling (a fine network of cracks in the enamel colours) is a good sign the piece is authentic. £500–800

SYMBOLS

The decoration on Chinese ceramics usually has symbolic significance:

Dragons represent authority, strength, wisdom, and the Emperor.

Pairs of ducks symbolize marital bliss.

The peony shows love, beauty, happiness and honour.

The pine, prunus and bamboo together denote spiritual harmony.

Cranes show longevity, and were traditionally a form of transport for Immortals.

JAPANESE POTTERY & PORCELAIN

Japanese ceramics have long been among the most sought after of all Oriental works of art. Although their wares often reflect the influence of Chinese styles, Japanese potters developed their own distinctive colour schemes and patterns. According to legend, the first Japanese porcelain was made in 1616, in the town of Arita, some years after it was first made in nearby China. The wares you are most likely to come across are Arita, Imari, Kakiemon and Satsuma. Not all of these cost a fortune – you can still find pieces for a few hundred pounds or less. Decoration can affect value dramatically. The plate below is worth over £12,000 because it is decorated with the cipher of the Dutch East India Company. Without this mark it would only be worth £1,500–2,000.

JAPANESE OR CHINESE?

Japanese blue and white wares, such as this c.1690 Arita export dish, have three distinctive features:

- granular porcelain material
- extremely dark (as here) or very soft underglaze blue
- three or possibly more spur marks, on the underside of the piece. £12,000–15,000

◀ ARITA WARES

Arita porcelain is named after the town of Arita, where Japanese porcelain production was concentrated. Although Arita, Imari and Kakiemon were all made in the same kilns, the term "Arita" usually only describes the blue and white wares produced.

▲ KAKIEMON WARES

Named after the man who is said to have invented coloured enamelling in Japan, you can identify Kakiemon wares, such as this dish, by their often geometric shape, white ground, high quality, often sparse, asymmetric, painted decoration, and a predominance of reds and sky blues. £10,000–12,000

▶ SATSUMA WARES

Satsuma wares are recognizable by their cream-coloured ground, lavish gold decoration, and finely crazed glaze. Prices vary widely – quality pieces may fetch tens of thousands, but you can sometimes find a single mid-19th century or later piece for as little as £100. This 19th century vase is one of a signed pair worth £3,000–5,000.

IMARI

Of all the types of Japanese ceramics, Imari (named after the port though which they were shipped to Europe) are the ones you see most frequently. This large late 17th century vase has many of the features characteristic of Imari wares.
£7,000–10,000

REMEMBER…
Remove loose lids from jars before you pick them up to examine them.

MANUFACTURE
Imari pieces were usually painted with dark underglaze blue decoration (see p63), glazed and fired, then enamelled with colours, gilded and fired again.

DECORATION
Floral designs or landscapes are usually set in shaped panels against the underglaze blue. Some pieces have figural knobs.

COLOURS
Colours typical of Imari are dark blue, iron-red and gilding, with an outline of black. The touches of green on this vase indicate its high quality.

CONDITION
Condition is crucial to value. However, damage can usually be restored and buying a slightly damaged piece can be an affordable starting point if you are on a limited budget.

TYPES
Large display wares such as this vase, which is designed to stand on a mantelpiece, are keenly sought after. Pieces in pairs and sets of three (called garnitures) in particular always command premium prices.

FAKES AND COPIES
Chinese potters made imitation Imari from the early 18th century and, later, European versions were made in Holland, Germany, Venice and Britain. These copies are valuable in their own right. Modern copies, like this Korean vase, may be expensive but have little status as collectables.

EARLY ENGLISH POTTERY

Love it or hate it – the naivety of early English pottery leaves few indifferent to its charms and there are enough smitten collectors to make the rarest pieces extremely valuable. During the late 17th and early 18th centuries English pottery underwent a period of rapid development and an enormously varied range of new wares and decorative techniques were developed. Pottery is categorized by the type of material from which the body is made

SLIPWARE	ENGLISH DELFT	SALTGLAZE STONEWARE
*c.*1720 SLIPWARE BAKING DISH £12,000–15,000	*c.*1730 BLUE DASH CHARGER £12,000–15,000	18thC TWO-HANDLED CUP £1,500–2,000
HOW, WHEN & WHERE — Made from red or buff earthenware, decorated with white or coloured slip (diluted clay). Zig-zag, feathered and marble designs predominate. Produced in Staffordshire, Wrotham in Kent, Bideford, Barnstaple, Wales, Wiltshire and Sussex. Dates from the 17th to mid-18thC.	Made from tin-glazed earthenware in Southwark, Lambeth, Bristol and Liverpool. Primitive designs of figures, animals and floral subjects mainly painted in blue, white, yellow, green and manganese. Known as "delftware" from Georgian times. Dates from mid-16th to late-18thC.	White Devon clay and powdered flint added to earthenware to make light-weight white wares; salt thrown in kiln during firing formed glaze pitted like an orange skin. After *c.*1745 more use of *famille rose* type enamel colours to imitate Chinese porcelain. Made in Staffordshire, from mid-18thC.
WHAT TO LOOK FOR — Dishes and mugs. Named or dated wares, especially those of best-known maker Thomas Toft, who occasionally signed his wares on the front – no marks usually. Beware of skilful fakes.	Blue-dash chargers – (plates with blue strokes around the edge as in the illustration; often decorated with monarchs); barbers' bowls, pill slabs, flower bricks. Chips are acceptable. Not marked.	Figures and pew groups (very rare), loving cups, mugs, plates, jugs formed as owls, unusually shaped teapots (camels, houses). Usually no marks.

(such as earthenware, stoneware, creamware) and the type of glaze used (such as tin glaze or salt glaze). If you are thinking of collecting early English pottery it's a good idea to learn the difference between some of the most important, and most common, categories. Below are six types of pottery made before c.1770 (for post 1770 see p78), as well as pointers on what pieces you can expect to see and which are most sought after.

WHEILDON	AGATEWARE	CREAMWARE	
MID-18thC PUG £3,500–4,500	c.1745 AGATEWARE CAT £2,500–3,500	EARLY CREAMWARE TEAPOT c.1760 £1,500–2,500	
Mid-18thC Staffordshire potter, Thomas Wheildon, developed lead-glazed pottery for tablewares and figures; colours were limited to olive-green, brown, grey and blue.	Layers of differently coloured clays rolled together, sliced to build up mingled layers resembling agate and moulded into wares. Lead and salt glaze were variously used; made in Staffordshire during the 18thC.	Coloured earthenware with transparent lead glaze, developed by Wedgwood in the 1760s, also made in other Staffordshire potteries and in Leeds, Bristol, Liverpool, Swansea and Derby. May be enamelled, plain or pierced.	HOW, WHEN & WHERE
Well-modelled animals like this dog; unusually shaped wares, candlestick figures, cow creamers, cottages with figures. Tablewares are less expensive. Never marked.	Cats, as shown, tewares, jugs, coffee and chocolate pots, shell-shaped wares – inspired by contemporary silver; pieces with more than two differently coloured clays. Never marked.	Red and black enamelling by Robinson & Rhodes; wares marked "Wedgwood"; pierced wares which may be marked "Leeds Pottery". Moulded pieces such as cruets and centrepieces. Few creamwares are marked.	WHAT TO LOOK FOR

CONTINENTAL POTTERY

Most Continental pottery was made from an earthenware base, covered with a glaze to which tin oxide has been added, and is known as tin glaze. Tin-glaze pottery is given different names according to its country of origin. In Italy and Spain it is called *maiolica*, in France and Germany it is known as *faïence*, and in the Netherlands as Delft.

The richly coloured designs and motifs found on Continental pottery of the 17th and 18th centuries provided a popular source of inspiration for makers of the 19th century and later. Most of these later copies are highly decorative and collectable in their own right.

▼ SPANISH MAIOLICA

Shiny metallic lustre decoration, as on this rare 15th century dish, is a characteristic of Spanish pottery. Similar pieces were reproduced in Italy in the late 19th century by the Cantagalli factory – these copies were originally marked on the base with a singing cockerel. £10,000–15,000

▲ DRUG JARS

Maiolica apothecaries' drug jars were made both for display and for storage – hence their colourful decoration. Shapes vary according to the jar's original contents. Wet drugs were stored in bulbous jars with spouts like this, dry drugs were usually stored in straight cylindrical ones called *albarelli*. £8,000–12,000

▲ FRENCH *FAÏENCE*

This beautifully painted 18th century plate was made by one of the most prominent French factories – that of the Veuve (widow) Perrin. Many wares from this factory are marked "VP", but the mark is also seen on copies, so always check the quality of the painting – painters from the factory were sent to the French drawing academies. £800–1,200

◀ DUTCH DELFT

Tulips were a Dutch obsession and Delft tulip vases were made in simple cushion shapes like this. Others resembled elaborate pagodas, standing several feet tall. £5,000–7,000

BEWARE

Some genuine pieces of *maiolica*, *faïence* and Delft have fake inscriptions to make them seem more valuable: be suspicious if the calligraphy seems to lack fluidity and if you see any grey specks in unglazed areas – a sign the piece has been refired.

COPIES

Many honest copies were made in the 19th century, marked by makers such as Doccia, Molaroni, Maiolica Artistica Pesarese and Bruno Buratti – these are collectable but considerably less valuable.

CONDITION

Don't expect to find early *maiolica* in perfect condition, chips and cracks are commonplace and pieces are still valuable despite damage. The rim of this tazza has been replaced in parts but is still worth over £12,000 because the painting is of such high quality. However, you can still find smaller, less finely painted examples from as little as £800.

ITALIAN MAIOLICA

The surfaces of valuable Istoriato (story) dishes, such as this 16th century Urbino tazza, are used like the canvas of a painting to show a mythological or religious subject – this picture of Rebecca and Isaac is from a Raphael drawing.

COLOURS

As in most Italian *maiolica*, the colours that predominate are blue, yellow, orange, black and green. If a wider range of colours is used it may indicate the piece is of higher quality or later date.

CONTINENTAL PORCELAIN FIGURES

Ask a collector to name a European porcelain factory and the chances are the first one they'll think of will be Meissen. This factory is famous because it was the first in Europe to discover the secret of making hard-paste porcelain (in the early 18th century) and because of the high quality of its products.

Meissen began to concentrate on producing figures from c.1730, following the arrival of a young sculptor named Johann Joachim Kandler. Before long, Kandler's figures became even more popular than Meissen tablewares. As other porcelain factories sprang up throughout Europe, they too began producing figures in the style of Meissen – some of them even using the Meissen crossed swords mark to make their pieces even more tempting.

If you're a new collector you may find the differences between the figures made by the various factories are often so small as to be easily overlooked, but as you become more experienced, details such as the modelling, the shape of a base, the colours and the glaze can tell you by whom and when a piece was made. Don't be afraid to pick the figures up and look underneath for marks – but always remember to support them well in your hand when you do.

◀ MEISSEN
You may think this twisting figure of Harlequin, made c.1740, looks as if it's about to topple over – but the turning pose is typical of the best Meissen figures which are always full of movement.
£15,000–20,000

REMEMBER . . .
Crossed swords alone don't mean you have a piece of Meissen – this is the most commonly faked mark and was copied by Worcester, Minton, Bow and Derby – among others.

▶ VIENNA
The different colours on a figure can tell you where it was made. The combination of strong green, pale mauve, puce and yellow used on this group is typical of many Vienna figures produced c.1760–70.
£3,000–5,000

▲ FRANKENTHAL
Frankenthal figures, such as this one, are often high quality despite their rather stiff poses. Features typically found on Frankenthal pieces are:
- large hands
- doll-like faces
- arched edge to bases
- tufts of green moss.

£2,500–3,500

IS IT MEISSEN?

Is the figure made from white paste, perhaps with a slight grey tinge?

NO → • If it is slightly blue and smoky it might be made by Vienna.

→ • If it has a distinct grey tone it may be modern Meissen.

YES ↓

Is it obviously separately modelled from the base?

NO → • If it looks as if it is growing out of its base it could be Nymphenburg.

→ A *c.*1660 Nymph-enburg figure of Summer

YES ↓

Is the base covered with flowers and leaves?

NO → • If it has patches of moss it could be Frankenthal.
• If it has a rough base or triangular gilt patterns it might be Vienna.

→ • If it has an undulating base with gilt or puce scrolls it might be Frankenthal.

YES ↓

Is the face severely modelled but subtly coloured?

NO → • If the features are very childlike it could be by Hochst.

A Hochst group
*c.*1700
£3,000–5,000

YES ↓

Is the painting very detailed, using either bold or pastel shades?

NO → • The colours on 19thC Meissen are often washed out and lack the fine details of the best 18thC pieces.

YES ↓

Is it marked with crossed swords on the base, the back or the side?

NO → • If there is no mark it could be an early figure by Vienna.

IF ALL THE ANSWERS ARE YES, THEN YOU MAY HAVE A PIECE OF MEISSEN.

MARKS OF OTHER MAKERS

▲ Hochst
◀ Frankenthal

▲ Nymphenburg

COMMEDIA DELL'ARTE

1 2

3 4

1 Scaramouch
2 Harlequin
3 L'Avvocato
4 Columbine

One popular subject for porcelain figures were characters from the famous *Commedia dell' Arte* (Italian Comedy). These were modelled by many factories and appear in a wide variety of poses. Their value depends on the quality and their condition, rather than the subject. Prices range from under £300 to over £20,000.

CONTINENTAL TABLEWARES

There are many different ways to build up an interesting and attractive collection of Continental porcelain. You might decide to concentrate on the wares of one particular factory, or a particular type of ware, coffee cups for example, which can still be bought singly and affordably. Alternatively, you may want to concentrate on pieces with a common style of decoration, perhaps painted with landscapes or flowers.

Whatever aspect you choose, you will find Continental porcelain in a huge range of styles, shapes, colours – and prices. Value is largely a matter of four key factors: maker or factory, style, quality of workmanship and condition. Identification is usually a matter of recognizing the characteristic features of each factory's wares such as the shapes, colours and type of paste and glaze they used. It is the combination of these factors, together with the mark (if there is one), which can tell you whether a piece is genuine or not.

▶ **CONDITION**
All these unusual Meissen vegetables have had some restoration, and this has reduced their value (to about £600 for the artichoke or the pair of peas). In perfect condition they would be worth about twice as much.

▲ **DECORATION**
Decoration can give away the maker's identity – Middle

Eastern figures, as seen on this plate, are typical of the Paris factory. £1,200–1,800

▶ **STYLES**
Dating some types of Continental porcelain can be confusing because during the 19th century factories like Sèvres often repeated earlier shapes and decorative styles. This Sèvres tea service uses shapes which were first fashionable in c.1790, but it was in fact made in 1837. £7,000–10,000

COPIES

Some copies are very skilful and are collectable in their own right. One of the most famous 19th century copyists, Edmé Samson of Paris, made this copy (left) of a Meissen original (right). You can tell it's a copy by the greyish colour of the porcelain, the heavier weight, and less lavish gilding. Copy £400–600; original £8,000–12,000

BEWARE

It's a great mistake to attach too much importance to marks, because many were copied – more than 90% of the Vincennes/early Sèvres linked Ls appear on later copies. One way of detecting fakes is by looking at the paste from which the piece is made – most copies are on hard-paste, but the original mark was used only for soft-paste (see p62 for how to tell the difference).

▶ SÈVRES

This Sèvres jug can be dated by the distinctive pink known as "*Rose Pompadour*" (after King Louis XV's mistress, Madame Pompadour). This colour was introduced *c.*1757 and was probably discontinued shortly after Madame Pompadour's death in 1764. £3,000–4,000.

COLOURS

Certain colours are associated with particular factories or periods. Some rare colours increase value.

1 Greyish turquoise: Meissen, *c.*1770
2 *Bleu Celeste*, Sèvres
3 Apple Green, Sèvres
4 Böttger Green, early Meissen
5 Lemon yellow, Meissen *c.*1730–50
6 Egg Yolk, Meissen *c.*1730–40
7 Tan, German and Swiss factories
8 Russet, Fürstenberg, Ludwigsburg
9 Dark brown, German factories
10 Iron red, all factories
11 Purple, Meissen
12 Claret, Vienna
13 Puce, German factories, *c.*1750
14 *Rose Pompadour*, Sèvres, 1760s
15 Lilac, Meissen, *c.*1740–55

EARLY ENGLISH PORCELAIN

When compared with lavishly decorated Continental wares, early English porcelain may seem relatively unsophisticated – but to many collectors this simplicity is fundamental to its appeal.

English makers tended to be much slower than their Continental counterparts in discovering how to make porcelain. One of the first English porcelain factories – Chelsea – was established by a French silversmith, Nicholas Sprimont in *c*.1745, nearly half a century after porcelain had first been made in Germany and France. Wares made by Chelsea were mainly intended for the luxury end of the market and are among the most sought after of all English porcelain.

Among the other famous names which were established at the same time as Chelsea, or soon after, are Bow, Bristol, Worcester and Derby. These factories produced many different types of wares and the best way of learning how to recognize the wares of each is to study and handle as much porcelain as possible. This way you will become familiar with the styles, colours, glazes and shapes used. As with almost any type of porcelain, marks are often spurious – they can be a help but should never be relied upon.

▲ BOW
Bow, which was the largest porcelain factory in mid-18th century Britain,

specialized in Oriental-style wares, like this tureen, which has features typical of most Bow pieces:
- white chalky paste
- greenish glassy glaze
- heavy potting.
  £4,000–6,000

◀ DERBY
English figures are usually more primitively modelled than those made on the Continent and tend to be less expensive. This Derby figure is worth £800–1,200.

MARKS

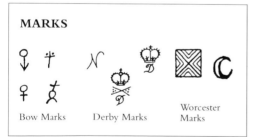

Bow Marks   Derby Marks   Worcester Marks

LOOKING AT PORCELAIN
Never pick up a piece of porcelain by the handle – it might come off. Support the main body firmly with both hands.

▶ WORCESTER
Hold a piece of Worcester up to the light and you should see a greenish tinge, perhaps with small patches of pinpricks. The moulded cabbage leaf decoration on the handle of this jug is typical of Worcester. £1,500–2,500

CHELSEA

Chelsea botanical plates of the 1750s are called "Hans Sloane" wares because the designs were based on prints of flowers from Sir Hans Sloane's Chelsea Physic Garden.

The shadows given to the insects are a device copied from Meissen and make them stand out more dramatically.

A typical feature of Chelsea is the way the specimens are painted on a larger scale than the flowers.

Chelsea wares can be distinguished from most other botanical plates because the flowers take up almost the entire surface of the plate.

CHELSEA MARKS

Chelsea wares are divided into groups according to the four marks used during the life of the factory. This plate, marked with a red anchor, dates from *c.*1752–57.

   Triangle period 1745–49
Raised anchor period 1749–52
Red anchor period 1752–57
Gold anchor period 1759–69

Despite a small crack, the high-quality painting makes this one of the most valuable types of botanical plate, worth £8,000–12,000.

BEWARE

Fake red and gold anchor marks are usually much larger than the genuine examples.

LATER ENGLISH POTTERY

Not only is the pottery of the 19th century colourful and decorative, it can often provide you with a fascinating visual record of the major events and personalities of the Victorian age. Firms such as Pratt & Co. perfected colour transfer printing from *c.*1840 and pot lids, boxes, plates and other wares were decorated with images of the royal family, the Crimean War and the Great Exhibition. Royal events such as Queen Victoria's wedding, the coronation and jubilees inspired a huge number of specially decorated wares. Many of these were originally sold for a few shillings but are now avidly sought after. Other highly popular collectables from this period include Staffordshire figures, blue and white transfer printed wares, Wemyss ware and ironstone. If all these are too expensive, look out for 19th century tiles – you can still find a Victorian printed version for £20–50.

▲ PRINTED BLUE AND WHITE POTTERY

Value depends on condition and pattern: because these three meat plates are all slightly damaged, they are moderately priced between £200–400 each. Less sought–after patterns start at around £120; the most valuable may be £2,500 or more.

◀ WEDGWOOD

Coloured objects, such as this 1780s moulded "Jasperware" vase, were made by dipping the object into slip (diluted clay). These wares were also made throughout the 19th century and later. However, the blue used in the19th century tends to be darker while 20th century copies are of lesser quality, £500–800.

▲ DINNER SERVICES

This Mason's Ironstone dinner service is made of a heavy earthenware substance first patented in 1813. It is usually easy to identify wares made by this factory as they're nearly always marked. The details of these marks changed over time; If the word "Improved" appears it means the piece was made after *c.*1840.

● Large dinner services are especially sought after and valuable. £4,000–6,000

WEMYSS WARE

Wemyss pigs such as this were made in Fife, Scotland, from 1880. There is also a wide range of Wemyss mugs, vases, jugs and jam pots, all of which have risen greatly in value recently. This pig is probably worth more than £800.

WHAT TO LOOK FOR

- good-quality painting
- tablewares with red borders – these are early
- figurative subjects – especially cockerels, cats, bees and pigs
- large pieces.

STAFFORDSHIRE FIGURES

Colourful creamware and pearlware figures, such as this spaniel, were produced on a huge scale in the late 18th century and throughout the 19th century. Some were made in Scotland and Wales but the majority came from the Staffordshire Potteries, so all examples of this type are known as Staffordshire figures;

nearly all examples are unmarked so the style of each should be carefully examined.

PAINTING

The detailed painting of the dog's face is a sign of quality and indicates an early date – later figures are more simply painted.

VALUE

Subject matter and rarity affect the price – figures of animals and royal, political and military subjects are particularly desirable. The spaniel would be worth around £1,200.

REPRODUCTION OR FAKE?

Less valuable Staffordshire figures were reproduced throughout the 20th century, often from the same moulds as genuine Victorian pieces. Even though genuine figures are often highly individual, these copies can be identified in several key ways:

Genuine
- crisp modelling
- detailed painting
- colourful decoration
- finger marks inside – from press moulding
- heavy thick walls
- erratic, widely spaced crackling in glaze
- soft gilding
- kiln grit and glaze on foot

Copy or Fake
- soft definition
- little detail
- little colour
- smooth inside – from slip casting
- thin fragile walls
- regular, exaggerated crackling in glaze
- bright gilding
- glaze wiped from foot

19TH CENTURY ENGLISH PORCELAIN

Various exciting new porcelain-making techniques were introduced and perfected in the 19th century. The development of bone china, which was made from the same ingredients as hard-paste porcelain (see p63) with large quantities of animal bone added, meant that less expensive porcelain became widely available.

Practical, relatively inexpensive dinner, dessert and tea services were made in large quantities, many of them embellished with printed decoration, which was also developed at this period.

You can still buy simple transfer-printed flat wares and hollow wares quite inexpensively. Some of the most affordable collectables are those made by the Goss factory during the second half of the 19th century. Statuettes and ornaments with printed decoration made by this factory are available for under £50.

BEWARE
Don't confuse hand-painting, which increases value, with hand-enamelled print (as seen on the left), which is generally less desirable. If it's hand-enamelled you will probably be able to see the transfer print underneath the enamel.

▲ PRINTED CHINA
Although hand-painted wares are usually more desirable than those with transfer-printed decoration, there are some exceptions. This teapot shows Queen Victoria and Prince Albert – a royal subject always pushes up the price and this would be worth £600–800.

◀ ROCKINGHAM
You may think this is a strange teapot but in fact it's a violeteer – a pot to hold petals and herbs. The highly elaborate moulded and flower encrusted decoration is typical of this factory. £500–800

◀ SPODE
Spode was one of the first factories to use bone china. You can recognize earlier (pre-1830) pieces by their mark, which was usually hand painted – later it was printed. Features typical of Spode porcelain are:
● pattern number in red
● very thin potting
● thin, smooth, white glaze. £1,200–1,800

At the other end of the spectrum, important factories such as Rockingham, Spode and Minton made a variety of highly ornamental wares, often using lavish gilding, elaborate, high–relief floral decorations and new techniques such as *pâte-sur-pâte*. Value is usually a matter of decorative appeal. Expect to pay more for hand-painted decoration. Any elaborately decorated piece will usually command a premium.

HOW TO DATE 19TH AND 20TH CENTURY PORCELAIN

"Royal" in trademark	after 1850
"Limited" or "Ltd" after name	after 1860
"Trade Mark"	after *c.*1870
"England" in trademark	after 1890
"Bone China"	20th century
"Made in England"	20th century

▼ MINTON

One of the most sophisticated innovations introduced by Minton during the 19th century was the technique of *pâte-sur-pâte*. This process was a laborious one which involved applying many layers of white slip (a mixture of clay and water) to a dark body which was then hand carved to expose the dark ground. The pieces were often decorated with lavish gilding and were always expensive; this *pâte-sur-pâte* vase would be worth £3,000–5,000.

◀ COALPORT

French designs of the 18th century became popular again in the 19th century. One of the most famous factories to make porcelain in the style of Sèvres was Coalport, who also copied the styles of Dresden and Meissen. This vase is particularly desirable because of its high–quality hand-painted birds. £1,200+

● Coalport is often marked AD1750. This is the date the company was founded, not the date of production.

▶ PARIAN

Although this elegant figure looks as if it's carved from marble, it's actually made from Parian, a type of porcelain. Parian figures became popular in the mid-19th century; the best were made (and marked) by factories such as Worcester (as this one is), Copeland, Belleek or Wedgwood and are well detailed. Unmarked figures are much less valuable. £1,000

The production of silver has a long and distinguished history, encompassing all the major decorative art styles. As a result, collectable silver is available internationally in a wide variety of forms. It is therefore perhaps unsurprising that, despite the vagaries of fashion, old silver has remained one of the most enduringly popular collecting areas. Although silver is not cheap, small 19th century objects are still available for £100 or less, and old Sheffield plate and electroplate also offer excellent value.

From the earliest times silversmiths realized that pure silver was unworkably soft, and had to be mixed with other more resilient base metals before it could be made into objects.

A silver standard was introduced in Britain in 1300 and all silver objects made after this date had to be tested and marked to show they contained more than 92.5% pure silver. This marking system has survived in Britain and Ireland with few modifications to the present day. Marks provide the collector of such silver with an invaluable aid. You may come across silver with fake or altered marks, or unmarked pieces, but these are relatively scarce, and once you have learnt to "read" the marks, you will be able to identify where, when, and often who made most pieces of silver. Nonetheless, you should always take into account the style of a piece to make sure it is consistent with the date of the marks. Much Continental and American silver was also marked in some way, although in many countries the system was less rigorously applied.

BASICS

HALLMARKS

There are four main marks:

- The sterling guarantee
- The town mark
- The date letter
- The maker's mark

Sterling guarantee mark

1 Leopard's head
2 Leopard's head crowned
3 Lion passant

Silver that is at least 92.5% silver is termed "sterling" silver. All silver objects of sterling quality were stamped with a leopard's head from 1300. By 1478 the leopard had a crown; from 1544 the sterling mark changed to a lion passant, shown walking to the left (after this date the leopard's head was used as London's town mark).

4 Britannia mark
5 Lion's head

Between 1697 and 1720, a higher standard of silver, known as the Britannia standard, was introduced. During this period the sterling mark was replaced by a figure of Britannia, and a lion's head in profile.

Town marks

Marks showing the town of assay were introduced by the end of the 15th century. Common marks are:

6 London
7 Birmingham
8 Chester
9 Dublin
10 Exeter
11 Edinburgh
12 Glasgow
13 Sheffield
14 York

Date letters

15   16   17   18

15 1721 16 1781
17 1741 18 1801

Marking with a date letter, which changed each year, was introduced in 1478 in London, and later in other parts of the country. The letters usually follow an alphabetical sequence, but the dates they indicate are unique to each assay office. The letters are contained within a shield of variable outline.

19 20

21 22

Maker's marks
19 Matthew Boulton
20 John Café
21 Robert Hennell
22 Paul Storr

Marks to show the identity of the maker were used from the 14th century. The earliest were pictorial symbols, but from the late 17th century marks increasingly incorporated the silversmith's initials.

ALTERED AND FAKE MARKS
Forged marks
Fake marks which have been added or "let in" to a piece are often incorrectly placed and may look distorted; if they have been made by recasting a genuine piece there may be small granulations visible in the outline.

Transposed marks
Marks are sometimes taken from a low-value object and inserted in a larger, potentially more valuable one. If you breathe on transposed marks you should be able to see a faint outline around the marks where they were soldered in.

Illegal alterations
An Act of 1844 made it illegal to alter any piece of silver without hallmarking the additions. However, many pieces were updated to make them more useful, or more fashionable, rather than to deliberately deceive.

PATINA
Over years of use, silver develops a soft glow, or patina, caused by accumulated scratching and knocks and bruises. This patina is important to value. Repolishing old silver on a buffing wheel can destroy the patina of a piece and is always considered undesirable.

WEIGHT
Although an item which is heavier than average may not appear much larger or heavier, any extra weight is usually synonymous with quality, and heavier pieces tend to be more valuable.

STYLES OF DECORATION
Silver styles reflect the taste of the period, and can often provide a good indication of date. Decoration may be applied to the surface or the border of a piece and usually adds to value (see p93 for some of the different types found).

CONDITION
Restoration work is usually detrimental to the value of a piece of silver. If lead has been used in the repair it can be especially unsightly. Always find a specialist silversmith if you decide a piece needs to be repaired. Areas particularly vulnerable to damage are:
- **Feet:** these can be pushed up through the base with time.
- **Handles:** the metal of the body may be pulled away by the handle.
- **Hinges:** can be broken and are often difficult to repair.
- **Pierced decoration:** may be relatively fragile and prone to damage.

SHEFFIELD PLATE
Sheffield plate, made from a fusion of copper and silver, was introduced in c.1740. Most Sheffield plate is unmarked, although some late 18th century pieces had marks very similar to those found on silver.
- A piece with "Sheffield plate" stamped on it is most likely to be electroplate made in Sheffield in the 19th century, and not genuine Sheffield plate.
- Sheffield plate tends to be much less expensive than solid silver, but the best pieces are still keenly collected.

ELECTROPLATE
This method, involving covering a base metal with a thin layer of silver by electro-deposition, was used from c.1840. The base metal was initially copper, but later nickel was used, hence the term EPNS (electro-plated nickel silver). Electroplate has a harsher, whiter appearance than sterling silver or Sheffield plate and is usually marked by its maker, or bears indications of quality.
- Apart from pieces by an eminent maker like Elkington & Co. who pioneered the process, electroplate is less collectable than other types of silver.

TEAPOTS, COFFEE & CHOCOLATE POTS

Tea, coffee and chocolate became fashionable in the late 17th century, and over the next two centuries large numbers of pots for serving these drinks were made.

The shapes of tea and coffee pots can help with dating them, but because many 18th century styles were repeated in the 19th and 20th centuries you need to check the marks on the base as well to tell whether the piece is a later reproduction. There is nothing wrong with buying, say, a 19th century coffee pot in an 18th century style, provided the marks are correct for the date it was made and the pot is priced as a reproduction. Bear in mind that coffee and teapots were made to be used and many have become well worn as a result – before you buy one examine it carefully for damage, which can be expensive to restore.

MARKINGS
Teapots are usually marked on the base – it's less common to find marks on the side. The maker's mark on a handle may be different from that on the body, as handles are nearly always later replacements, particularly if they are made of silver. Lids should also be marked.

▲ TEAPOTS
The "bullet" teapot has a lid with a concealed hinge, which was attached before the base was soldered on. Check lids carefully before buying – if the hinge is weak it may be impossible to restore. £4,000+

◀ DECORATION
Decoration can help with dating. This piece shows a technique known as bright-cutting, which was popular in the late 18th century. £1,500–2,000

WHAT TO LOOK FOR
- Check the point where the handle joins the body to make sure it's secure.
- Examine the hinge on the lid – check it is not weak or restored
- Make sure the spout isn't split.
- Breathe on the finial and around the spout and hinges – this helps to show repairs.

◀ STYLES
Some 19th century teapots were so elaborately decorated it is hard to imagine they were ever used! This one, made in 1814, is covered with undulating foliage and has a handle made to look like bark. £1,500–2,000

COFFEE POTS

This 1734 coffee pot could have been used either for coffee or chocolate, but pots which have a removable finial, with a hole in the lid to insert a swizzle stick for stirring the sediment are usually termed "chocolate pots.". Some examples were even produced with matching stands and burners, all of which should bear the same marks.

PAUL DE LAMERIE

One of the most acclaimed silversmiths of the 18th century, Paul de Lamerie, was a Huguenot (a French Protestant) and a political refugee who built up a prosperous London business. De Lamerie's clients included royalty and his most famous pieces were very lavishly decorated.

MAKERS

The mark of a well-known maker can add enormously to the value of any piece of silver – this pot was made by Paul de Lamerie, so it would be worth over £30,000; a similar pot from a lesser known maker would cost £5,000–7,000.

● Other famous and collectable names to look out for are: the Batemans, the Barnards, the Fox family, Robert Garrard & Co. and Paul Storr.

MARKS

These should be in a line by the handle, or in a group, or scattered on the base. Lids should also be marked.

ALTERATIONS

During the 19th century, covered tankards, such as the one on the left, became unfashionable and were sometimes converted into the much more popular coffee pots. Converted pots, such as that on the right, are illegal unless the additions are marked.

MUGS AND JUGS

A huge variety of cups, tankards and jugs have been made over the centuries. They remain highly popular with today's collectors. The vast majority of those you are likely to come across today date from the 18th century or later. Although silver is relatively robust, jugs and mugs have often been well used and condition is important to value – so examine pieces carefully before buying them.

Other factors which affect the value of mugs and jugs are common to any type of silver – namely quality, date and maker. You will find that a mug marked by a known maker will invariably cost more than an unmarked one. Elaborate decoration will also raise the price – although take care because many once plain 18th century tankards (lidded mugs) were elaborately decorated in the Victorian period and these are less desirable than a plain piece in original condition.

	MUGS	TANKARDS
	BALUSTER MUG *c*.1740 £1,500–3,000	**EARLY 18TH CENTURY TANKARD** £4,000–5,000
WHEN AND WHY	Made from the late 17thC, early mugs mirror the shapes of pottery – with bulbous bases and slender necks. Those made in the early 18thC had straight tapered sides; later the baluster shape became popular. Mugs became fashionable as christening gifts in the 19thC.	Most date from *c*.1600–1780. Made for drinking ale, they became less prevalent as wine and spirits became more popular. Georgian tankards are usually plain; some have armorials. Tankards made in the 19thC (often for presentation) were usually very elaborate.
WHAT TO LOOK FOR	**Marks:** until the end of the 18thC, in a group under the base; later pieces are marked in a line by the handle. • Check handles and rims for signs of weakening or splitting. • Examine sides for signs of erased armorials (see p89)	**Marks:** on one side of body or base and on lid; earlier tankards have marks in a line on top of the lid; later they are in a group inside. • Check handle sockets; they may have become weak. • Examine thickness of cover – if it's domed, and thin, it may have been reworked from a flat lid.
OTHER STYLES		

BEWARE

Tankards were often converted into more useful jugs during the19th century. To be legal the conversion must have later marks on any parts which were added – such as the spout. This jug was once an 18th century tankard but it was converted and decorated in the Victorian period. Pieces which have been converted from other forms usually have less elegant proportions than authentic originals. £1,500–2,000

JUGS

CREAM JUG, 1730
£1,500–3,000

SAUCEBOATS

GEORGE III SAUCEBOAT, 1761
£3,500–4,500

Made from the 16thC for shaving or for serving liquids such as beer, wine, water, milk or cream. Earlier jugs occasionally had hinged lids, but by the mid-18thC many small open jugs on three legs were made for serving milk or cream.

Earliest date from *c.*1710 and have a spout at each end and two handles on either side of the centre. Later, shallow jug-like sauce boats with central pedestal feet were popular. Three small feet were used in mid-18thC, after which central bases returned to favour.

WHEN AND WHY

Marks: should be on the base or on body, near handle, or under spout. Lidded jugs should have a full set of marks on the body and a maker's mark and lion passant only on the lid – a full set of marks on the lid means it was probably once a tankard!
- Beware of soldering around the spout – it could indicate a less valuable conversion.

Marks: usually underneath in a straight line; those made in the 1770s sometimes have marks under the lip.
- Check legs aren't bent or pushed through the body.
- Examine handles (they can be vulnerable).
- Look at rims – these can be split.
- Pairs – they are worth at least three times the value of singles.

WHAT TO LOOK FOR

OTHER STYLES

CADDIES & CASTERS

Don't be shocked by the extravagance and the cost of the caddies on this page – tea was once so expensive that it was drunk only in the wealthiest homes, and the caddies for storing this precious commodity were intended as objects for display as much as for storage. Caddies were usually kept in the drawing room; some had detachable caps for measuring the tea, while others were even fitted with a lock and key to protect their precious contents from dishonest servants! Nowadays, caddies are keenly collected – and the finest examples can be expensive.

Casters also played an essential role in fashionable dining rooms as liberal quantities of spices and seasonings were essential to disguise the flavour of stale food. Early casters had straight sides; baluster casters were made from *c.*1705, becoming taller during the century. Most were originally made in pairs or sets and today these are always particularly sought after.

▶ CADDIES

Sets of caddies always command a premium. This set of two caddies and a sugar box would be particularly valuable because each piece has its original arms and it comes complete with its fitted box.
£10,000–15,000

▲ MARKS

The bodies and lids of caddies should have a full set of matching hallmarks, although early 18th century pieces with detachable lids, such as this one, are often unmarked on the cap.
£2,500–3,500

WHAT TO LOOK FOR

This caddy has three key features you should look out for on other pieces:
- high-quality decoration
- unworn condition
- date marks of the 18th century – 19th century caddies are usually less valuable. This particular one is worth about £2,500–3,500.

▲ CASTERS

Sugar casters first appeared in sets of three; one large caster for sugar, and two smaller ones for dry mustard and pepper. The shape of casters changed little from *c.*1705. Better quality ones, such as this, have elaborately pierced covers. This is one of a set made by David Tanqueray in 1713 and is worth over £5,000.

SALVERS & TRAYS

The difference between salvers and trays is that trays have handles while salvers do not. Both were used as presentation pieces as well as for practical purposes, and good examples are always popular with collectors. Many salvers survive from *c*.1700 onwards, but trays were not made until the end of the 18th century. Those that are decorated with elaborate borders will probably cost more than simpler ones.

Salvers and trays often had the armorials of their owner engraved in the centre – if the crest belongs to a well-known family it can increase the item's value – as well as providing an interesting insight into the previous owner of your tray.

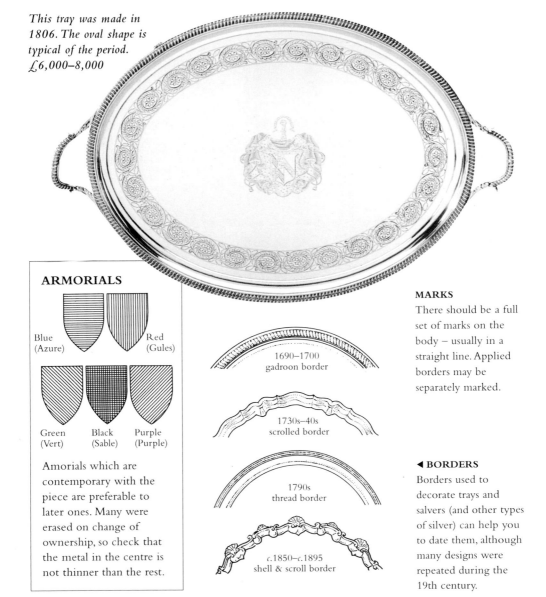

This tray was made in 1806. The oval shape is typical of the period.
£6,000–8,000

ARMORIALS

Blue (Azure)

Red (Gules)

Green (Vert)

Black (Sable)

Purple (Purple)

Amorials which are contemporary with the piece are preferable to later ones. Many were erased on change of ownership, so check that the metal in the centre is not thinner than the rest.

1690–1700
gadroon border

1730s–40s
scrolled border

1790s
thread border

c.1850–*c*.1895
shell & scroll border

MARKS
There should be a full set of marks on the body – usually in a straight line. Applied borders may be separately marked.

◀ BORDERS
Borders used to decorate trays and salvers (and other types of silver) can help you to date them, although many designs were repeated during the 19th century.

FLATWARE

Knives, forks and spoons are usually termed "flatware" by silver collectors. Depending on your budget there are a number of different ways to collect flatware. Complete services, which usually comprise settings for 12, are rare and so may seem prohibitively expensive, but odd numbers of spoons and forks in the most common patterns, such as Old English, Fiddle, or Hanoverian are relatively easy to find, and it's often far less costly to build up a service piecemeal. Flatware services do not usually include knives. These often had thin metal blades which can quickly become worn; as a result most collectors prefer reproductions, which are more robust.

▶ APOSTLE SPOONS

Produced from the mid–15th century, Apostle spoons (so-called because the handle is decorated with the figure of an Apostle) are among the most valuable of spoons. These are sometimes faked by reshaping ordinary 18th century spoons – you can spot these by the stiffness of the figure and the later marks, if they remain. £1,000+

▼ PATTERNS

Different patterns are easily identifiable by their names; below are some examples of the most popular ones which have been repeated continually since they were first made and are still in use today. The date of a piece of flatware can affect its price even more dramatically than other types of silver.

1 Rat-tail **2** Old English **3** Fiddle end
4 Beaded **5** Albany

▲ OLD ENGLISH PATTERN

The most desirable flatware services contain a dozen tablespoons, table forks, dessert spoons, dessert forks and teaspoons. This 77-piece Old English pattern service has the added bonus of a basting spoon and other serving pieces and this will increase its value.
£6,000–8,000

BEWARE

Badly worn flatware is virtually impossible to restore and is worth only scrap value. Only the fork on the left is in good condition. The one in the centre is badly worn, the other has been trimmed to disguise the damage.

CANDLESTICKS

Even though we no longer depend upon candlelight for illumination, nothing graces the dining table more elegantly than a pair of silver candlesticks. Most candlesticks and candelabra were originally made in pairs or larger sets. Expect to pay more than double for a pair of candlesticks than you would for two singles – even if they're the same design and size! To be a true "pair" candlesticks must be the work of one maker and of more or less the same date.

This typical mid-18th century candlestick was made by casting the separate sections – base, stem (or column), sconce (or capital) and nozzle – in moulds. Cast candlesticks are usually more desirable than *"loaded" ones, which were made from thin sheets of silver with an iron rod down the inside, and filled with pitch to give weight. A pair of cast candlesticks like this would cost £3,000+.*

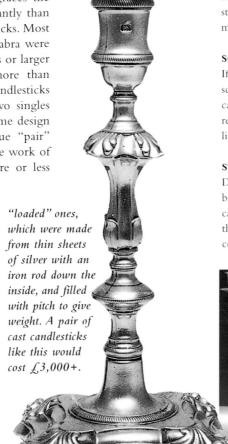

NOZZLES
Nozzles – which hold the candle and stop wax dripping down the stem – should have the maker's mark and a lion passant.

SCONCES
If the seam on the stem and sconce is not in alignment, the candlestick has been heavily repaired. Here you can see the lion passant mark on the sconce.

STEMS
During the 18th century stems became progressively taller; early candlesticks rarely measure more than 13cm/7in; this mid–18th century one is 25cm/10in.

BASES
Sheet candlesticks are marked in a line above the base, cast ones are marked in the well, or under each corner.

◀ CHAMBER CANDLESTICKS
These were used to light the way to bed and, unlike other candlesticks, are usually sold singly. This one was made in the 1780s and, like many of its kind, is fitted with its own snuffer.
£1,000–1,500

▲ CANDELABRA
The separate parts of a candelabra are frequently replaced – four nozzles on this pair are replacements, but these examples were made by John Scofield, an eminent 18th century maker, so the price would still be £15,000+.

MISCELLANEOUS SILVER

If you want to collect on a modest budget, the vast array of small novel objects made from silver can provide an ideal collecting area. Look carefully in the display cabinets of a general antiques shop, or at a silver auction, and among the pieces you are likely to find individual items such as pincushions, card cases, nutmeg graters, vinaigrettes, snuff boxes, sewing cases, glove stretchers, letter openers, vestas and sovereign cases – to name but a few! When you examine the marks you'll find Birmingham's anchor mark appears again and again because from the late 18th century silversmiths in this area produced small silver items in their thousands. Usually, the less expensive pieces tend to be those produced during the 19th century; earlier objects are scarcer and can be highly priced.

▶ SNUFF BOXES

The decoration of small boxes has a huge bearing on their price; hunting scenes are particularly sought after – this silver gilt snuff box, made in 1828, would be worth over £1,500+.

▶ VINAIGRETTES

Vinaigrettes such as these were used to contain aromatic salts, vinegar or perfume and are smaller than snuff boxes, although equally in demand. £1,500–2,000

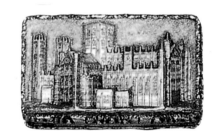

▶ DECORATION

A piece of silver decorated with a recognizable scene is especially desirable. This Victorian pin tray shows Windsor Castle – one of the most popular views; St Paul's Cathedral or scenes of Edinburgh are also keenly collected. £800–1,200

WHAT TO LOOK FOR:

Silver boxes
- Check the hinge isn't damaged.
- Make sure the marks on the base are the same as those on the lid – if they don't match, the box may have been altered.

BEWARE

Sometimes snuff boxes are turned into vinaigrettes by adding grilles – just as vinaigrettes are sometimes turned into pill boxes by removing their grilles! £200

▶ **MIRRORS**
Like most silver-framed
mirrors, this one is part
of a set of dressing table
silver. Its unusually fine
quality is reflected in
the high price it
commands – over
£100,000 for the set!
During the late 19th
and early 20th century
other less expensive
mirrors were made
from wooden frames
covered with velvet
and decorated with
die-stamped silver.
These are often badly
worn and can be very
difficult to clean but
are still sought after.

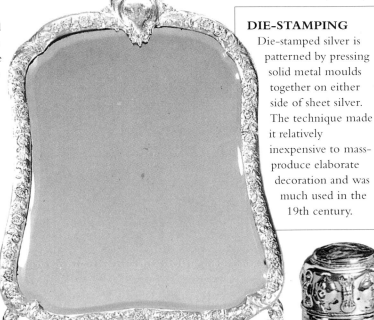

DIE-STAMPING
Die-stamped silver is
patterned by pressing
solid metal moulds
together on either
side of sheet silver.
The technique made
it relatively
inexpensive to mass-
produce elaborate
decoration and was
much used in the
19th century.

▲ **SILVER AND
GLASS**
Glass and silver are
often combined to
produce some highly
decorative objects;
particularly dressing
table accessories, but
before you decide to
buy a silver and glass
object remember to
check that the glass
is not broken because
it can be costly to
replace, especially if
shaped. This 1911
Ramsden & Carr silver
and enamel case still
contains its original
glass bottle. £2,000+

▲ **ART NOUVEAU
SILVER**
Silver items reflecting
the Art Nouveau style,
marked by well known
makers or retailers, are
becoming increasingly
collectable. This box,
with its typical Art
Nouveau motif on
the lid, was made for
Liberty & Co. and
would be worth
£800–1,200.

SILVER DECORATION
Small silver is decorated in a wide
variety of ways. Some of the most
common terms used to describe the
techniques are:
Bright-cutting: a type of faceted
engraving.
Chasing or Embossing: patterns
made by hammering or punching tiny
marks onto the silver.
Card-cut decoration: flat shapes
added to handle mounts, etc.
Filigree: open wire panels decorated
with little silver beads.

OTHER METALS

Pewter, brass, copper, Sheffield plate and electroplate are just a selection of the most commonly seen metals that have been used to make a wide variety of decorative and utilitarian objects throughout the centuries. Dating unmarked metal objects can be a potential minefield if you're not sure what to look out for. The style of a metal object rarely provides a reliable way of deciding when it was made because many early designs were copied in the 19th and 20th centuries.

Before you make a purchase don't be afraid to pick up different pieces to compare their weight: most modern copies are noticeably lighter in weight than genuinely old ones. Look for signs of wear and tear consistent with age: the undersides of objects should be covered with a fine patina of scratches and edges of plates and hollow wares should be worn smooth. Treat anything with sharp edges or which looks as though it's in perfect condition with suspicion.

◀ PEWTER

Pewter, or "poor man's silver" as it is sometimes known, is an alloy mainly made of tin and lead, in varying proportions. Prices range from around £800, although pieces in poor condition are less desirable. This *c.*1780 flagon has an attractive acorn finial and domed cover typical of the period, as well as "wriggle-work" decoration, and is worth £2,000–3,000.

HOW OLD IS IT?

- Pewter more than 50 years old develops a characteristic dull glowing patina through polishing and continual use.
- Fine-quality pieces made before *c.*1826 are usually marked with a maker's stamp and a crowned X mark showing the purity of the metal.
- Tavern pewter made after *c.*1826 should bear capacity marks.

▲ BRASS

Old brass objects, such as this George III candlestick, often reflect the decorative styles of silver objects from the same period. Pieces marked with maker's stamps are especially desirable and command a premium; this candlestick is marked by the famous maker E. Berry, and so a pair would be worth £1,000–2,000.

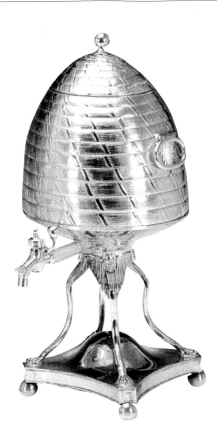

◀ SHEFFIELD PLATE
Old Sheffield plate was made from a thin layer of silver fused onto a sheet of copper. This type of plate was used from *c*.1760 as a less expensive alternative to silver. Although highly collectable, Sheffield plate remains good value; this *c*.1810 novelty tea urn is worth £800–1,200.

● You can usually identify old Sheffield plate by its slightly pinkish tinge caused by areas of silver wearing thin and revealing the copper body beneath.

▶ COPPER
If you find a piece of metalware marked with a twisted rope symbol you're in luck because this is factory mark of leading 19th century manufacturers Perry, Son & Co. This unusually-shaped Perry jug is doubly desirable as it was also designed by Dr Christopher Dresser, one of the most influential designers of the Victorian period.
£1,500–2,500

▲ ELECTROPLATE
● The technique of applying a thin layer of silver over a nickel or alloy base was developed in the mid-19th century.

● Electroplate is very susceptible to wear – you can see how the silver has worn thin on parts of this corkscrew.
£300–500

● You can always have pieces replated but this gives an unnaturally bright appearance which is generally considered far less desirable.

Antique glass is a fascinating and accessible collecting area. Despite the fragility of the substance, glass from the 18th century and later is relatively easy to find, and plain objects can still be inexpensive.

Although the precise origins of glass production are unknown it was certainly made in ancient Egypt, Syria and Rome. The method by which the basic material is made is very simple: A silica (usually sand) is heated with a flux (potash or soda) and a stabiliser (usually lime) until it fuses together.

One of the most obvious objects to collect are antique drinking glasses. Made in large numbers throughout the 18th century, these have long been popular with collectors. Value depends on the rarity of the decoration, as well as the shape of the bowl, stem and foot. Many of the more valuable types of 18th century glass have been faked so always try to buy from a reputable source and take expert advice when in doubt about a purchase.

The colourful glass produced in the 19th century is also becoming increasingly popular with some collectors. Many new glass-making techniques were introduced during this period as were a number of new colour variations. Two of the most attractive 19th century types to look out for are cameo glass and overlay glass, although the best examples, those marked by famous makers, can be expensive. Despite this growing popularity, unmarked glass from the 19th century is still available at reasonable prices, and 19th century table glass can sometimes be less expensive than modern equivalents.

BASICS

The body of a glass item is known as the metal. The colour and texture of the metal change according to the ingredients used. There are three main types of glass:

SODA GLASS

Also known as *cristallo*. Made in Venice from the 13th century. The soda was derived from the ashes of burnt seaweed, and gave the molten glass a malleable quality which allowed glassmakers to create very elaborate shapes.

POTASH GLASS

Called *waldglas* in German. Potash glass was first made in Bohemia in Northern Europe. The potash was derived from burnt wood and bracken. Potash glass is particularly hard and is well suited to cutting and engraving.

LEAD GLASS

Made from potash with the addition of lead oxide (instead of lime), this glass, developed by George Ravenscroft, was used in England and Ireland from the late 17th century, and in Europe from the late 18th century. Lead glass is characterized by its weight and clarity and is well suited to cutting.

DECORATION

Decoration which has been added onto glass can add substantially to its value. The main decorative techniques used are:
- Cutting
- Enamelling
- Gilding
- Engraving

CUTTING

Cut facets in glass emphasize its refractive (light-transmitting) qualities. Cut decoration can help with dating. The earliest patterns were shallow surface cuts. Patterns became increasingly elaborate in the late 18th and early 19th centuries (see p100–101).

An 18th century enamelled wine-glass attributed to William Beilby £4,000–6,000

ENAMELLING

Painting in coloured enamels was popular on Venetian glass from the late 15th century and became fashionable in England in the mid-18th century. The best-known English enamellers were the Beilby family. There are two types of enamelling:

- **Fire enamelling:** the enamel was painted on the surface of the glass, and the glass fired to fix the decoration. This is the most permanent and usual form of enamelling.
- **Cold enamelling:** also known as cold painting, involved painting the glass without firing. This technique has the disadvantage that the enamelling wears off easily, and was mainly used on inexpensive items.

GILDING

Gold decoration can be applied to the surface of glass in a number of different ways. The most permanent method of gilding is by firing the gold onto the surface of the glass. An alternative method was oil gilding, which involved applying a gold powder or leaf onto an oil base and then burnishing. Gilding applied using this method is easily rubbed off.

ENGRAVING

Engraving was first introduced by Roman glassmakers It is used to add both patterns and scenes. There are four types of engraving:

A diamond-etched wine glass. Dutch, 17th century. £1,400–3,200

Diamond point engraving: the design was scratched onto the surface of the glass using a tool with a diamond nib. This technique was used in the 16th century in Venice, and in Britain in the late 16th century.

Wheel engraving: the design was engraved using small copper wheels of varying diameter, which rotated against the surface of the glass, and an abrasive. The method was widely used in Germany in the 17th century, and became the most

common form of engraving in Britain from the 18th century.

A stipple engraved glass, Dutch, c.1745. £2,500–3,500

Stipple engraving: a fine diamond needle was tapped and drawn on the surface to form a design built up from dots and small lines. This technique was popular in the Netherlands during the 18th century and is also found on English glasses.

Acid etching: this technique involved covering the surface of the glass with varnish or grease, and scratching the design with a needle or sharp tool. The surface was then exposed to hydrofluoric acid which etched the design on the glass.

This method was popular in the 19th century.

AUTHENTICITY

Fakes of many of the more expensive types of antique glass abound. Victorian glassmakers made imitations of 18th century glass and many fakes have also been produced in the 20th century. These are often discernible in four key ways:

- **Colour:** the distinctive tint caused by impurities may not be present in reproductions.
- **Manufacturing method:** hand-blown glass usually has a pontil mark – a rough bump under the stem – where it was cut from the pontil rod. It may have striations of ripples in the glass and the rim may be of uneven thickness. Later machine-made glass does not have these imperfections.
- **Proportions:** glass has varied in style and proportions throughout the centuries. On old glasses the foot is usually as wide as the bowl, or slightly wider. The wrong proportions may indicate a fake.

DRINKING GLASSES & DECANTERS

When compared with antique ceramics of the same date, the majority of antique glass remains relatively inexpensive. You can still find sets of 19th century glasses for under £150 at antiques shops and general auctions, and incredibly, an antique decanter will often cost less than a modern one.

During the 18th century, large numbers of drinking glasses were made in many different styles. The variety still available means that there are lots of possibilities for collecting glass. You may decide to focus your collection on, say, glasses with air twist stems, Jacobite glass, cordials, or gilded glass, or you may prefer to simply collect single examples of each type as they catch your interest. Simpler 18th century glasses may cost as little as £80–120, but very elegant examples, or those with elaborate or particularly unusual decoration can be much more valuable.

SIGNS OF AGE
- A conical or funnel bowl
- a foot that is wider than the rim
- flaws in the glass and a slightly irregular body indicating it was handmade
- a bumpy "pontil mark" under the foot
- a greenish or greyish tinge in the glass
- signs of wear on the foot – fine and irregular scratches.

JACOBITE GLASSES
Glasses engraved with roses, doves and oak leaves were made in the 18th century to show furtive allegiance to the Old Pretender (James Edward Stuart) and the Young Pretender (Charles Edward Stuart). Jacobite glasses are particularly collectable but can be expensive – an especially rare one was sold in 1992 for £66,000.

◀ COLOUR TWISTS
Stems with threads of coloured glass are keenly sought after; value depends on the number of colours. This one has blue and opaque white twists, and would be worth about £1,800.

▶ GILDED GLASS
Glasses with original, soft 18th century gilding, such as this one, are very desirable, but are rarely seen in perfect condition. £600+

BEWARE
You can spot less desirable later gilding by its harder, brighter appearance.

Collectors categorize and assign value to drinking glasses according to the shape and decoration of the bowl, stem and foot. This one is of medium quality – it has a plain round funnel bowl and a relatively simple knopped stem, but because it is larger than most 18th century glasses (measuring 22cm/9in tall) it is worth slightly more than usual. £600.

This is a multi-knopped stem, so-called because of the series of projections with which it is decorated; some stems have only one knop, which may contain a tear drop of air, other stems are decorated with air twists.

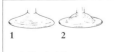

1   2   3

1 Multiple spiral

2 Single series

3 Double series.

1   2

1 Conical foot

2 Domed foot

This glass has a domed foot, a feature which is characteristic of many early glasses; others have conical feet. Check the edge of the rim for unevenness, as this may mean a chip has been ground down.

The bowl of this 1720 glass is a round funnel shape; other bowl shapes are show below.

1 Bucket
2 Waisted bucket
3 Conical
4 Bell
5 Ogee
6 Trumpet

DECANTERS

Decanters were often decorated with engraved or gilded labels describing their contents. This one is made from "Bristol" blue glass – an area associated with coloured decanters, although not all were made there. £250–350

CUT & PRESSED GLASS

Nothing makes glass sparkle more brightly in candlelight than cut decoration, and this is one reason why cutting has long been one of the most popular ways of embellishing all types of glass objects. Early glass was simply cut by hand, in fairly shallow patterns, but gradually patterns became deeper and designs more elaborate, and by *c.*1830 mechanized wheel cutting became the norm. In the 19th century production increased as new techniques for machine-made, press-moulded glass – which looked like cut glass but was much quicker to produce – were developed in America.

Although 18th century cut glass has increased in popularity and price; it can still be good value. If you want to collect cut glass to use on the dining table rather than simply for display look out for sweetmeat dishes, jellies, custards, fruit bowls and candlesticks; many of these are still relatively inexpensive, especially if you buy them singly.

▶ IRISH GLASS

If you see a piece of glass which looks rather lopsided the chances are it's Irish! Glass made in Ireland, such as this bowl, can also often be identified by its greyish tinge and the typical shallow diamond cutting of the decoration. £800

CUT OR PRESSED?

Cut glass is usually far more desirable and valuable than pressed glass, and there are several ways of identifying it:

- sharply faceted decoration
- no mould lines along the inside
- irregular thickness.

CUT GLASS PATTERNS

These are some of the most common cut glass patterns used during the 18th and 19th centuries. However, because they have been repeated in the 20th century, the pattern alone is not a reliable guarantee of authenticity – you should also look at the colour of the glass, and for flaws in the metal and slight irregularities in shape that show it is handmade.

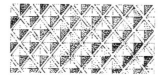
Plain sharp diamonds

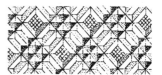
Strawberry diamonds

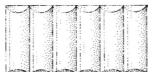
Pillar flutes

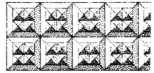
Cross-cut diamonds

Star cutting

Fine diamonds

THE HANDKERCHIEF TEST

Plain early glass has sometimes been decorated with later engraving to make it seem more valuable. To check the decoration is authentic, drop a white handkerchief in the glass – old engraving will look dark and grey, new engraving white and powdery.

- A handkerchief is also useful to reveal the colour of the glass.

▲ PRESSED GLASS

During the Victorian period clean and coloured pressed glass plates were often made to commemorate important events; this one celebrates Queen Victoria's Golden Jubilee. £30–40

▼ LATER CUT GLASS

Extensive sets of less elaborate turn of the century cut glass can still be very affordable. This is a selection from a set of 89 items made c.1900; the whole set would cost about £400–600.

◀ ROCK CRYSTAL

Engraved lead glass, cut and polished to simulate the natural facets of rock crystal, is known as "Rock Crystal" and became popular during the 19th century. £300–400

COLOURED GLASS

Coloured drinking glasses and decanters were produced in relatively small quantities in England during the 18th century. However, many 18th century styles were copied in the late 19th/early 20th century and some later versions are so convincing that even more experienced collectors can be confused.

Most of the coloured glass you are likely to come across dates from after c.1800, when many lavishly decorated glass objects were made in Britain, on the Continent and in the United States.

WHAT TO LOOK FOR

- Pieces marked by the workshops of Thomas Webb, W.H.B. & J. Richardson and Stevens & Williams (now Brierley).
- Larger pieces.
- Unusual shapes – particularly for ornamental pieces.
- Multiple layers of glass.
- High-quality design – Neo-classical figures are especially desirable.

◀ OPALINE GLASS
Although at first glance this goblet looks as though it's made from porcelain, it's actually an example of English opaline glass made c.1850. Much opaline glass was also made in France; quality can vary – the best pieces are made from lead crystal and are very heavy.
£400+

▶ CAMEO GLASS
Cameo glass – made by overlaying the base colour with a layer of contrasting glass which was then carved to reveal the colour underneath – is one of the more expensive types of 19th century coloured glass. This large bottle is nicely carved and has a silver lid, so it is worth £1,500–2,000; but even miniature bottles would be worth £200.

▲ RUBY GLASS
Ruby glass, sometimes made from tinted glass or from clear glass with a ruby stain on the surface, was produced in both Bohemia and England. These pieces were made in England in the mid-19th century. The value of the piece on the left is high (£2,500–3,000) because of the elaborate silver gilt handles; the jug on the right is worth £500–700.

PAPERWEIGHTS

The most sought-after antique paperweights are those made by famous French factories such as Baccarat, Clichy and St Louis during the mid-19th century. Patterns were built up from tiny slices of different coloured rods or canes of glass, set in a mould and covered in clear glass. Sizes vary from under 5cm/2in to over 10cm/4in; unusual sizes, especially miniatures, are highly collectable.

BACCARAT
You can often identify the maker of a paperweight by the type of rods it contains and the way they are arranged. The rods in this example include silhouettes of a dog, a horse and a deer, all designs typical of the Baccarat factory. Other common Baccarat silhouettes include arrowheads and shamrocks. £6,500–7,000

BEWARE
Reproductions of antique paperweights abound, but can be identified by their lighter weight.

MILLEFIORI
Millefiori (meaning "thousand flowers") paperweights are so-called because their canes resemble a carpet of flowers.

IDENTIFYING MARKS
Baccarat paperweights often include signed and dated canes – this one is marked *B 1848*. St Louis and Clichy paperweights are also sometimes marked with initials.

▲ ST LOUIS
Large single flower heads were much used by the St Louis factory. Sometimes flowers were laid on a criss-cross lattice ground, usually in white or pink, known as *lattichio*. £500-600

▲ CLICHY
Clichy weights can often be identified by the characteristic rose they contain. This one would be worth over £2,000 but more common types fetch from around £400.

▲ OVERLAY WEIGHTS
Some rare weights, such as this one made by Baccarat, contain a layer of opaque glass through which windows are cut to reveal the design beneath. This particular example would be worth £3,000 or more.

Clocks have been appreciated and treasured from at least the 17th century to the present day. Unlike other types of antiques, clocks are unique in that they are "working" pieces. Sometimes described as "mechanical pictures", clocks can be appreciated both for their visual appeal and for their technical mastery. They also serve a more practical purpose in telling you the time.

If you're a novice collector thinking of investing in a clock, it's probably best to buy one that's in working order. Most clocks can be repaired, but restoring a "bargain" can be a laborious and expensive business, and unless the problem is very straightforward it's often cheaper in the long run to buy a clock which has been properly overhauled and restored to working order by a skilled clockmaker.

Most clocks are relatively easy to date and identify because the vast majority were signed by their maker on the dial and movement, and records of most makers have survived thanks to the tight control of the governing body, the Clockmakers Company, which was founded in 1631. Value depends on the maker, movement, case and condition, but a clock's visual appeal lies largely in its case, which usually reflects the furniture style of the period, but these are rarely signed and little is known about this aspect of the trade.

Despite their popularity, clocks are available at a wide range of prices. Plain carriage clocks are available from about £800, a simple bracket clock might cost £4,000, and a late 19th century longcase from £4,000.

BASICS

There are three key elements which you should assess before buying a clock;
● the mechanism, or movement
● the dial
● the case.

MOVEMENTS

The movement consists of a system of brass and steel wheels and gears, known as the train. It is usually housed between two brass plates.

The escapement: this part of the movement controls the speed at which a clock runs.

Verge or balance wheel escapement: the balanced wheel was used on lantern clocks until *c*.1670. The oscillating balance wheel releases the two pallets or "flags" on the vertical bar, which engage the toothed wheel. The verge escapement is similar but has a short pendulum.

Anchor escapement: this was first used in longcases from *c*.1670, and became standard for longcases and brackets. The anchor engages with the teeth of the escape wheel. Clocks with an anchor may have a long or short pendulum.

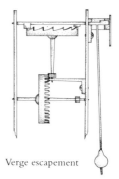

Verge escapement

Balance wheel

PENDULUM

Weight-driven and spring-driven clocks usually have a pendulum to control the clock's speed, which swings in a regular arc. The pendulum is a brass or steel rod with a metal disk, or bob, at the bottom (usually lead cased in brass). On a verge escapement the bob is usually on a threaded rod. On an anchor escapement, the bob slides on the rod and can be locked in place tightening a nut. Adjusting the position of the bob on the rod alters the timekeeping of the clock.

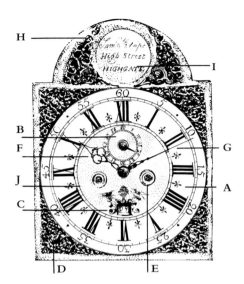

DIALS

A chapter ring
B subsidiary dial
C calendar aperture
D applied corner
spandrels
E winding holes
F hour hand
G minute hand
H dial arch
I engraved boss
J "matted" centre

The dial is the face of the clock and is attached to the movement by a number of brass "feet". A dial has an important bearing on price. Clocks with replaced dials are much less desirable. There are four main types of dial:

Brass dials: this is the earliest type of dial, used on lanterns, brackets and longcases.

Each one has the hours engraved on a seperate chapter ring.

Painted metal dials: found on most clocks after *c.*1800. These became increasingly elaborate in the 19th century.

Painted wooden dials: found on British dial clocks, tavern clocks and Continental clocks. If authentic, the wood should show some signs of cracking caused by changes in temperature.

Enamelled metal dials: common on carriage clocks and other types of French clock. They are made out of enamel which hase been fired on top of a thin copper sheet.

HANDS

Early clocks only have one hand (for hours), but from *c.*1660 most have a minute and an hour hand. Second hands are usually shown on a subsidiary dial. Hands are usually made from blued steel, although gilded brass is found from *c.*1790. Until *c.*1740 the hour hand was elaborate; the minute hand was longer and simpler.

● Replacement hands are acceptable if they are in the right style.

CASES

The case houses the dial and movement. Knowledge of materials and styles is useful in dating a clock and in assessing its value. In Britain and the United States, wooden cases were popular. Metal cases, or those combining materials are more likely to be Continental.

Wooden cases: these were introduced in the 17th century. Many cases are covered with thin veneers of wood. The most common woods are ebony, walnut, mahogany and rosewood. Wooden cases are sometimes decorated with inlaid marquetry (patterns made by using

different woods, see p44), lacquer, applied metal mounts, brass inlay (particularly on rosewood cases), or a combination of tortoiseshell and brass (known as boulle work).

Metal cases: brass is the most common metal; all carriage clocks are brass-cased. Old brass is uneven and shows marks left by the casting process; modern rolled brass is of uniform thickness. Brass cases may be elaborately engraved or decorated with enamel colours.

SIGNATURES

Most clocks are signed, although a signature is not always a guarantee that the clock was made by the maker whose signature it bears; 19th century clocks may be signed by the retailer rather than the maker. Genuine signatures are usually found in the following places:

● until 1690: along the bottom of the dial plate.
● from 1690–1720: on the chapter ring.
● after 1720: on the chapter ring; or on the boss in the arch or on a separately applied plaque.

BRACKET CLOCKS

Not all "bracket" clocks stood on wall brackets. Clocks of this type were also used for tables and mantlepieces. Nowadays the term is used to describe all clocks with short pendulums and spring-driven mechanisms. These clocks are also sometimes called "mantel clocks" or "table clocks".

Bracket clocks were made from *c.*1660, the earliest with square brass dials; by the beginning of the 18th century, arched dials became more common. Among the most

often seen British bracket clocks are those with mahogany veneered cases. Large numbers were produced from the late 18th and early 19th century, mainly in London, and you can still find clocks of this type for around £6,000–12,000. Also frequently seen are French 19th century clocks, which were made in a wide variety of shapes. Many of these incorporate such lavish decoration that you may need to take a second look before you realize they're clocks at all.

▼ EARLY BRACKETS
Early (pre-1700) bracket clocks, such as this *c.*1695 one, are usually the most valuable. You can generally identify them by their ebony, walnut or even olivewood veneered cases and elaborately decorated square dials.

▶ REGENCY CLOCKS
You can recognize a bracket clock made in the Regency period, as it will usually have a convex dial signed by its maker, simple hands made from brass or blued steel, and a mahogany or rosewood case. £6,000–10,000

MAKERS
The value of a clock is greatly increased if it's signed by a famous maker. The dial and backplate of this clock (above and right) are signed by Thomas Tompion, one of the most famous English clockmakers, known as the "father of English clockmaking", making it worth over £100,000+! Other famous names include the Knibb brothers and Edward East.

▲ FRENCH BRACKET CLOCKS
Depending on the degree of elaboration, prices for French clocks start at around £1,500. This one is decorated with a bronze figure of a Negress (representing Africa), a gilt panther and tortoises. It is therefore worth £8,000 or more.

MOVEMENTS
Most mahogany bracket clockss originally had a verge escapement (see p104–105); many of these were later converted to an anchor escapement but this should not put you off buying.

STRIKE/SILENT LEVER
The strike/silent lever controls the striking mechanism of the clock and can be used to turn it off without affecting its running.

MAHOGANY BRACKETS
Most mahogany clocks are larger than earlier ebony or walnut examples. This one, which was made c.1783, is of a standard size and measures 51cm/20in. £12,500

CLOCK CARE
- Carefully dust and wax wooden cases.
- Never attempt to clean brass or silvered dials.
- Ask an expert to oil and clean the clock's mechanism.
- Hold clocks upright if you are moving them from one room to another.
- Secure or remove the pendulum before a long journey.

BEWARE
Check the finials all match. On many clocks some have been replaced – this is less desirable.

CASES
Both elaborate and simple cases were made from mahogany. This example is fairly simple, but the six illustrations below show some of the more elaborate varieties.

Lacquer
*c.*1770
ht 63.5cm/25in

Mahogany
*c.*1780
ht 49.5cm/19½in

Mahogany
*c.*1780
ht 52cm/20½in

Mahogany
*c.*1795
ht 40cm/15⅞in

Ebonized
*c.*1810
ht 48cm/19in

Mahogany
*c.*1827
ht 66cm/26in

LONGCASE CLOCKS

Perhaps because of their homely appearance and reassuring "tick-tock" sound, longcases, popularly known as "grandfather" clocks, are among the most appealing of all antique clocks. Most longcases were made in Britain from the late 17th–19th centuries, although lesser numbers were also produced in Europe and the United States. The standard longcase runs for 8 days and has an anchor escapement. Like most types of clock, value is dependent on the quality of the case, movement and dial, and on the identity of the maker. If a clock has an unusual or attractively painted dial, or an elaborate marquetry or lacquered case, it will cost more than a run-of-the-mill version. Size can also have a bearing on price. Smaller longcases are usually more expensive than larger ones – and for good reason – taller ones were built to fit in rooms with much higher ceilings than are found in many homes today. So before you buy a tall longcase remember to check that it will fit!

DIALS

Originally only square, dial faces developed arches in *c*.1720. Most longcases have brass dials, as shown here, or painted ones, like the clock opposite. Brass dials are usually about 30cm/12in in diameter and have

an applied chapter ring (the band showing the numbers) and applied decorative spandrels (corners).

QUICK DIAL CHECK

Square
(17thC)

Arched
(*c*.1700–19thC)

Circular
(*c*.1800)

▲ **WALNUT LONGCASES**
Some of the earliest longcase clocks were decorated with walnut veneers over an oak carcass. Cross-banded veneers (short strips applied so that the grain lies at right angles to the main veneer) add to the value. £35,000+

▲ **MARQUETRY**
Floral marquetry was a popular decoration on longcases between 1680 and 1710. Earlier examples have small panels of marquetry inset in the veneer but are otherwise similar to walnut longcases; later ones, such as this, are much more lavishly decorated. £25,000+

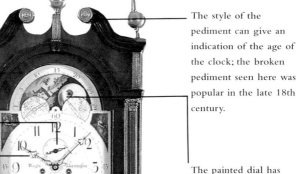

Finials are easily damaged and replacements, though acceptable, are less desirable.

The small dials measure the seconds and the calendar months.

The hands on most longcases are made from "blued" steel – the metal was heated to create the dark colour.

The trunk – centre section of the case – has a door which opens to allow you to adjust the pendulum and fit the weights. Longcases were designed to stand against a wall, so the backs are usually made from unpolished wood.

The style of the pediment can give an indication of the age of the clock; the broken pediment seen here was popular in the late 18th century.

The painted dial has attractive figures in the spandrels and a moon disc, showing the phases of the moon, in the arch. Look for crazing (a fine network of cracks) on painted dials as this is a sign of authenticity.

NAMES TO LOOK OUT FOR

This clock is signed by a Birmingham clock-maker named Edward White. London makers of longcases are usually particularly sought after, especially Thomas Mudge Sr., William Dutton and John Holmes.

MAHOGANY LONGCASES

Mahogany was used to make longcases from the mid-18th century until the early 19th century. This example, which was made in 1785, has a fairly elaborate case and it is worth around £6,000. However, you can still find simpler 19th century versions from about £4,000.

The wood used for the base and plinth should match the rest of the case. Variations in the colour and overall appearance may mean that parts have been replaced and this will reduce the clock's value.

CARRIAGE CLOCKS

Few people today would think of packing a carriage clock when they go on a journey, even though, as one of the earliest types of travelling clock, this is what they were made for. Carriage clocks usually have brass cases and were fitted with handles so they could be more easily carried – hence their name. Many also came with a leather travelling case. Nearly all carriage clocks were made in France during the 19th century and the early years of the 20th century; a few were also produced in England. Carriage clocks are among the least expensive types of antique clocks available. You can still buy less elaborate models for around £800–1,200 although good-quality ones may cost over £3,000.

CHECKLIST OF TYPICAL FRENCH CARRIAGE CLOCK FEATURES

- white enamel dial
- black numerals
- stamped mark or signature on the backplate
- 8-day duration spring-driven movement with going barrel
- bevelled glass panels
- blued steel hands.

QUALITY FEATURES

- engraved metal case
- panelled *cloisonné* (floral enamelled decoration) case
- porcelain case
- subsidiary dials.

FIRMS & MAKERS TO LOOK OUT FOR

Auguste (active from 1840), French
Abraham-Louis Breguet (1747–1823), French
Achille and Louis Brocot (active 19thC), French
Dejardin (active 19thC), French
Pierre and Alfred Drocourt (1860–89), French
Frodsham family (19th/20thC), English
Paul Garnier (*b.*1801–*d.*1869), French
Japy (1772(early 20thC), French
F. A. Margaine (*c.*1870–1912), French
E. Maurice (active 1880s), French
James McCabe (19thC), English
Soldano (*c.*1855–80), French

◄ REPEAT BUTTONS
Some carriage clocks have a repeat button on the top of the case: when the button is pressed the clock repeats the last hour struck. This one was made by Henri Jacot *c.*1890. £2,000–2,600

◄ ENGRAVED CASES
Engraved-case carriage clocks are more valuable than plain ones. Look for elaborate, detailed decoration which covers as much of the case as possible. This one was made by Le Roy & Fils *c.*1865. £5,000–6,000

◄ SUBSIDIARY DIALS
Clocks with smaller subsidiary dials are especially desirable. This English carriage has a seconds dial; some clocks have dials showing the days of the week, but the most common subsidiary dial is an alarm. £2,000

NOVELTY CLOCKS

Novelty clocks, which tell the time in a particularly unusual or intriguing way, are among the most fascinating of all clocks. The earliest novelty clocks date date back to the 17th century, but most of those seen today come from the 19th century when they were produced by several French, Swiss and British makers. The value of a novelty clock is dependent on its rarity, appearance and the complexity of any moving features, rather than the clock mechanism itself. Condition is also particularly important, as broken novelty clocks can be extremely complex and expensive to repair.

► MYSTERY CLOCKS

This is one of the most common types of novelty clock. The movement, concealed in the base, rotates the figure slightly from left to right, and this motion makes the pendulum swing, even though the figure holding it seems unconnected to the mechanism. £4,000

◄ AUTOMATON CLOCKS

Automaton clocks are among the most varied and valuable of novelty clocks. This one is relatively simple – it contains a bird which every hour sings a melodic nightingale song, while flapping its wings, turning its head, and opening its beak. £6,000–8,000

► SKELETON CLOCKS

The basic principle of the skeleton clock is to display as much of the working mechanism as possible. The origins of skeleton clocks lies on the Continent, but the most complex and elaborate pieces are English. This typically elaborate example (with protective glass dome removed) dates from c.1870, and was made by J. Smith & Sons. £9,000–15,000

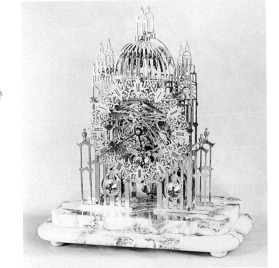

Rugs & Carpets

Contrary to general belief, the only difference between a rug and a carpet is size. Rugs are usually small enough to hang on the wall – up to 2m/6ft long – anything larger is usually referred to as a carpet. Broadly speaking, rugs and carpets fall into two main groups: serious collector's rugs and decorative rugs. Older rugs (over 100 years old) are usually only of interest to the specialist collector. More recently-made rugs and carpets are chiefly of interest to the decorative buyer.

Weaving and carpet-making are among the most ancient crafts and probably originated in central Asia. The oldest surviving fragment, called the Pazyryk Rug, was found in Siberia and dates from the 5th century BC.

Most rugs are categorized by their place of origin or the tribe who made them. To be able to identify the difference between, say, a Kazak and a Kuba, you need to familiarize yourself with the various distinctive colours, patterns, motifs and weaves characteristic of each type.

The size, richness of the colours, fineness of the knots, intricacy of design and condition are all important when valuing an antique rug. Collectable rugs should be handmade. To check, look on the reverse – you should be able to see the design on the back as well as on the front. Next, part the pile and look at the knots; if there are loops rather than knots this indicates a machine-made rug of very little interest to collectors. Many types of antique rug cost little more than modern replicas. Woven Kelims and Soumacs can be found for upwards of £300.

BASICS

MATERIALS

The foundation material of a rug (the warp and weft) is usually wool, cotton or silk. The best-quality wool is fine, soft and shiny. Inferior-quality wool is coarse and lacks lustre.

COLOURS

Colour is one of the most important factors in assessing old rugs. The best colours are those made from natural vegetable and insect dyes.

Natural dyes

Blues and reds predominate in most old rugs. Warm red colours are usually derived from the plant, madder. Blue comes from indigo.

- Sometimes crimson comes from insect dyes such as cochineal. This indicates a date after c.1850 when cochineal was first imported to the East.

Chemical (aniline) dyes

These were introduced c.1890; they tend to be harsher in tone, and are not colourfast.

Chromatic dyes

These were first used in the early 20th century. They can be difficult to distinguish from natural dyes as they are colourfast, but they lack the subtlety of natural dyes, and come in a wider colour range.

KNOTS

The type of knot used to attach the pile to the warp and weft can help to identify where it was made. The quality of a rug is reflected by the fineness of the knots, which are measured according to their number per square decimetre (15 sq. in). A coarse rug may have only 400 knots per square decimetre whereas a fine one may have many thousands. The knots are tied over the warps of the rug by hand and then cut to the correct length. Each row of knots is separated by one or more lines of weft beaten into place with a metal comb. Two main types of knot are used:

- Turkish, symmetric or Ghiordes; this was used in Turkey and by many tribal groups in Persia and central Asia.
- Persian, asymmetric or Senneh; used in Iran and by some central Asian groups. The threads can be open to the left or right.

PERSIAN RUGS

Richly coloured and exotic, Persian rugs have long been highly sought after; the finest are made from silk and are among the most expensive of all Oriental carpets. Most Persian carpets seen today date from the 19th and 20th centuries and can be either tribal village pieces woven both for trade and for use, or town-made factory woven pieces, produced specifically for the Western market.

CARPET CARE

Carpets can be washed with plain warm or cold water and a mild detergent. Snow is a good way of removing dust – cover the rug with snow and brush it off and it will take the dust with it!

◀ PRAYER RUGS
Garden motifs recur in many Persian rugs and are inspired by the Islamic notion of the garden of Paradise. Prayer rugs – small carpets used to kneel on during prayer – such as this late 19th century one, show the garden through a *mihrab* or arch.
£800–1,800

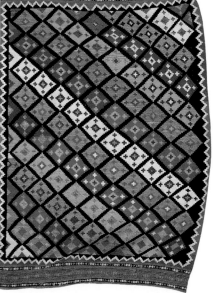

▶ KELIMS
Unlike other types of carpets, Kelims are flat-woven which means they have no knots and no pile. Traditionally made entirely from wool there are many modern reproduction kelims on the market, identifiable by their bright colours and coarse weave. Old or antique rugs like this Qashqai kelim from the late 19th century, are finely woven and softly coloured. £800+

▲ CONDITION
The town of Heriz in northwest Iran was a prolific centre of carpet production. This Heriz carpet has areas of repiling, and the outermost borders at each end have been cut and bound; even so, because of its attractive pattern, unusual and sought-after ivory coloured field and good size – 4.35m x 2.97m /168in x 114in – it would still cost over £6,000.

CAUCASIAN & TURKISH RUGS

Distinctive geometric designs are a keynote of many types of Oriental rug made in the region between the Black and Caspian Seas. In this rugged mountainous area, known as the Caucasus, carpets were made by villagers using small looms. Each different region has its own distinctive characteristics. Among the most famous and frequently seen Caucasian rugs are Kazaks, Shirvans and Soumacs.

Turkish carpets fall into two distinct groups: those made by nomadic tribal weavers and those made in urban or Imperial factories. Rugs cover a wide spectrum of prices, from expensive silk rugs to cheaper Anatolian kelims, which are still available for a relatively modest outlay.

▼ SOUMACS
Soumacs are a type of kelim and are one of the easiest of the Caucasian rugs to identify because they are flat-woven rather than knotted, but, unlike other kelims, are patterned on one side only, with the weft left uncut for warmth. This is a Soumac bagface – trappings such as bags, saddle covers and tent hangings are always popular with collectors and can be surprisingly expensive. £400+

▲ KAZAKS
Large, bold geometric patterns and long, fine-quality wool are features of Kazak rugs. They are usually relatively small – this one is 150 x 113cm/5ft x 3ft 9in and is worth £1,500–5,000.

KAZAK MOTIFS

Pinwheel   Karachov   Fachralo   Bordjalou

Kazaks are often named according to their distinctive designs. These are some of the most commonly seen motifs.

WHAT TO LOOK FOR
- bright vibrant colours – preferably coloured with vegetable dyes (see p112)
- finely textured weaving
- good condition, unless very early
- complete rugs – cut down ones are less desirable
- a natural patina.

IS IT OLD?

- Check the pile with a magnifying glass. If the fading is soft and gradual it's old; if you can see three distinct bands of colour the rug may be artificially aged.

- Lick a handkerchief and rub it on the carpet – dyes which come off copiously may be chemical – an indication that the carpet is not of great age.

WHAT DO COLOURS MEAN?

RED	happiness
BLACK	rebellion and devastation
BROWN	plentitude, fruitfulness
WHITE	cleanliness, serenity, purity
GREEN	rejuvenation
GOLD	prosperity

▶ LADIKS

The central Anatolian village of Ladik is renowned for its fine-quality prayer rugs (see p113). This one contains a poetic inscription at the base of the niche. £5,000+

◀ SHIRVANS

Shirvans typically have fine knots, short pile and small geometric patterns, in which dark blues and strong reds predominate. £1,500–3,500

MODERN RUGS

Modern rugs, such as this Shirvan, are coloured with synthetic dyes which look harsh compared to naturally dyed rugs. Modern Shirvans can also be identified by their longer pile and cotton warp and weft. Although they are still of interest to the decorative buyer they are far less valuable. This one is worth £300–500.

INDIAN & CHINESE RUGS

A prison may seem an unlikely setting for valuable carpet-making, but during the 19th century large numbers of woven and pile carpets were made in Indian jails such as Agra, Amritsar and Hyderabad and today these are extremely sought after. Indian piled carpets, first made in the 16th century for the Mongol rulers, often reflect the influence of Persian rugs which were used as a source for some designs. India is also famed for its flat-woven *dhurries* – the Indian equivalent of kelims.

The real and imaginary beasts and symbols of power, wealth and good luck which pepper the surface of many Chinese rugs make them highly distinctive – and easy to recognize. Most of those you are likely to come across date from the 19th century or later and were specially made for the Western market.

VALUE POINTS

- Pile Agras are among the most valuable of Indian carpets – prices range from £20,000-70,000.
- In Indian carpets, white or yellow grounds are usually more valuable than red or blue, which are more common.
- *Dhurries* are the least expensive of Indian carpets; prices range from £500-2,000 for a large one.
- Chinese carpets are also fashionable at the moment. Those made in the 19th century usually fall in the £3,000–15,000 price range.
- Post-World War II Chinese carpets that drew on French designs and look less "Chinese" are not as valuable as traditionally patterned ones.

▲ INDIAN CARPETS
Carpets made in India for the European market were often extremely big. Large rectangular carpets are usually more sought after than square ones. This Agra measures 600 x 424cm/19ft 8in x 13ft 11in. £30,000–50,000

▼ CHINESE CARPETS
Traditional motifs seen in Chinese art provided the inspiration for patterns on rugs made in China. The design of this Ninghsia rug was probably adapted from contemporary brocade. £5,000–10,000

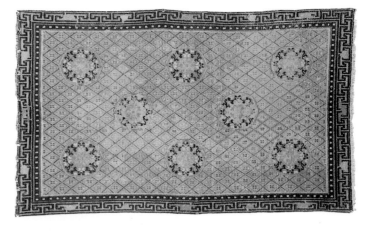

EUROPEAN RUGS

If you visit a sale of Oriental rugs or a specialist carpet dealer, you may be surprised at the large number of European-made carpets on offer. Carpet-making was introduced to Europe by Moorish invaders in the 8th century. Among the most popular and abundant Western rugs are needlework rugs. Many were made by ladies of the leisured classes from the 16th century onwards, but some were commercially produced during the 19th century. Designs are colourful and extremely varied; some patterns were adapted from Oriental rugs, others were derived from printed textiles.

Flower-filled rugs from the Aubusson region of France have also enjoyed a huge upsurge in popularity. If the price of an Aubusson is out of your reach, you may be able to find slightly worn small rugs or fragments for more modest sums.

AUBUSSON RUGS
The most sought after Aubussons, such as this example, made c.1890, were flat-woven on a loom (although some piled examples are known). £15,000

PATTERN
The design was built up one colour at a time, each colour woven back and forth only in the area required. When a new colour was added a vertical split was left between the wefts, which was stitched up by hand afterwards.

BORDERS
The border of this Aubusson has been cut or folded back and the design along one edge has been distorted as a result. Aubussons were originally made with very wide plain borders and were intended to fit right up to the walls and to be cut to fit around fireplaces.

NEEDLEWORK RUGS
The pleasant floral design, good condition and gentle, yet unfaded, colours are all signs of a good-quality rug. Such traits add to the desirability of this mid-19th century needlework rug and mean that it is worth around £5,000–10,000.

Art Nouveau & Art Deco

Art Nouveau and Art Deco are two of the most significant movements to emerge in the last years of the 19th and early 20th centuries. The appearance of furniture and applied arts of this period was dramatically altered by these new styles which swept through Europe, Britain and the United States.

"Art Nouveau" derives its name from a shop in Paris, *La Maison de l'Art Nouveau*, which retailed glass and furniture designed by such innovatory figures as René Lalique, Emile Gallé and Louis C. Tiffany. The style first appeared in Belgium *c.*1892 before spreading to France at the end of the 19th century. Most Art Nouveau objects are characterized either by sinuous fluid forms derived from nature or, particularly in Britain, by simple straight-lined designs with a heavy vertical emphasis.

"Art Deco", named after the 1925 Paris *Exposition Internationale des Arts Décoratifs et Industriels Modernes*, embraces two very different approaches to the applied arts. On the one hand, French designers made luxurious objects of the highest quality in exotic woods. On the other, modernists like the Bauhaus in Germany developed clean simple shapes suitable for mass production using the "new" materials like tubular steel and chrome that were becoming available.

In the middle years of the 20th century Art Nouveau and Art Deco became rather unfashionable but today almost any type of object reflecting these styles is highly collectable, although prices for many small mass-produced objects are still relatively low.

FURNITURE

Art Nouveau and Art Deco furniture covers a wide spectrum of quality and prices. The most sought-after and valuable pieces are large, commissioned handmade items, by known designers. Smaller functional objects, such as writing desks, chairs and original mass-produced furniture, are widely available and relatively inexpensive.

▶ CHARLES RENNIE MACKINTOSH
One of the most influential British Art Nouveau designers, Charles Rennie Mackintosh, usually designed his furniture to commission. The clean simple lines of this chair are in stark contrast to the fluid forms of most French Art Nouveau furniture.
£100,000

◀ LIBERTY
Furniture made for the influential firm of Liberty & Co. is usually marked with a Liberty label and despite being highly collectable it can still be affordable. This dressing table is part of a set which also includes a pair of wardrobes; the whole suite would be worth about £3,000.

▼ EMILE GALLÉ

This small table, designed by Emile Gallé, one of the leading French exponents of the Art Nouveau style, has five features characteristic of most Gallé furniture:

- strong sculptural quality
- inventive design
- fruitwood marquetry inlay
- stylized floral decorative motifs
- a signature.

It is worth £7,000–10,000.

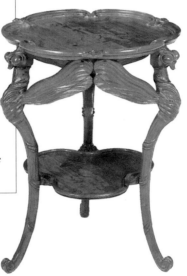

BEWARE

Pieces marked GALLÉ which lack the originality of earlier designs and are less inventive in their use of inlay may have been made by Gallé's firm after his death. Although collectable, these are less valuable than pieces made in Gallé's lifetime.

WHAT TO LOOK FOR

Much unsigned furniture of the 1920s and 30s, such as this cocktail cabinet, remains relatively inexpensive. Quality can vary; you should look for:

- uncracked veneers
- original upholstery
- pale woods
- simple but dramatic geometric forms.

£1,500+

LUDWIG MIES VAN DE ROHE

One of van de Rohe's most popular Art Deco designs, Barcelona chairs such as this were first made in 1929 and have been mass-produced continuously since World War II. Pre-mass-production chairs are worth around £10,000 – ten times more than later versions – and can be recognized by:

- a bent chrome steel top rail with separate sections joined by lap joints and screwed with chrome-headed bolts
- a welded stainless steel rail along the top.

GLASS

Unlike most earlier glass (see pp98-103), the value of a piece of Art Nouveau or Art Deco glassware is dependent largely on its maker or designer. This was the heyday of influential glass makers such as Emile Gallé, Daum and Lalique in France, and Louis Comfort Tiffany in America. Designers no longer tailor-made their output of glassware primarily for the dining table. Glass was increasingly used to make a plethora of decorative vases and new electric lamps and, spurred on by the new requirements of "modern" life, designers produced objects as diverse as car mascots, jewellery and scent bottles. All named glass of this period is widely collected, and the best pieces are very expensive, but you can still find some unmarked pieces or smaller objects for relatively modest prices.

◄ GALLÉ GLASS
The best pieces, such as this lamp, are made from hand-carved cameo glass (formed by fusing two or more layers of coloured glass, the top layer carved to reveal the colours underneath). Later machine-made versions are less valuable and are identifiable because the carving is not so deeply cut. £15,000+

◄ DAUM FRÈRES
Daum glass, such as this vase, is often very similar to that made by Gallé but can usually be identified by a gilt signature *DAUM NANCY* on the black enamel on the underside. £3,000

FAKES
Fake Art Nouveau glassware abounds. Among the objects most likely to deceive are:
● "Tiffany" lamps – with fake marks identifiable because they do not usually have the marked pad on the shade.
● Cameo glass marked "Gallé" recognizable by its stiff, lifeless decoration.

MARKS
Gallé pieces are usually marked with a cameo or incise-carved signature. If you see a star after the signature, the piece was made during the first three years after Gallé's death, between 1904 and 1907.

► TIFFANY
Tiffany lamps have bronze or gilt bronze bases; the shades are made from a lattice of bronze, set with small pieces of favrile (iridescent) glass. They are marked on an applied bronze pad. £10,000+

LALIQUE

All types of glass made by the most famous glass designer of the Art Deco period, René Lalique, are highly collectable. His prolific output included car mascots, clocks, lighting, jewellery, furniture and figurines. Lalique's distinctive wares were also much imitated so before buying something which you think could be by Lalique ask yourself the following questions...

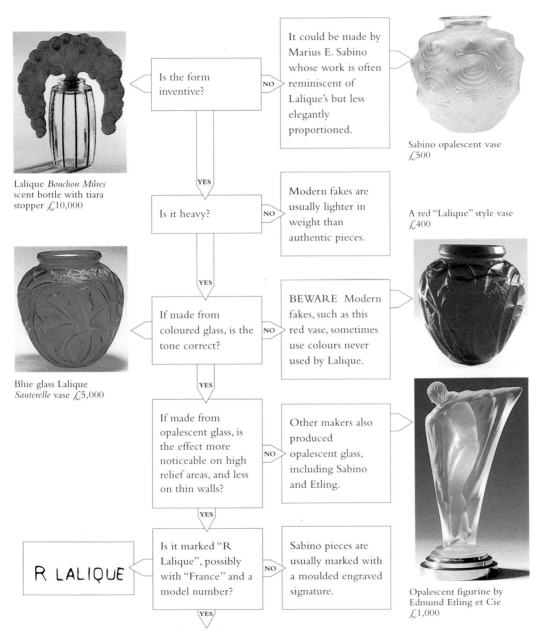

Lalique *Bouchon Mûres* scent bottle with tiara stopper £10,000

Is the form inventive?

NO — It could be made by Marius E. Sabino whose work is often reminiscent of Lalique's but less elegantly proportioned.

Sabino opalescent vase £500

YES

Is it heavy?

NO — Modern fakes are usually lighter in weight than authentic pieces.

A red "Lalique" style vase £400

Blue glass Lalique *Sauterelle* vase £5,000

YES

If made from coloured glass, is the tone correct?

NO — BEWARE Modern fakes, such as this red vase, sometimes use colours never used by Lalique.

YES

If made from opalescent glass, is the effect more noticeable on high relief areas, and less on thin walls?

NO — Other makers also produced opalescent glass, including Sabino and Etling.

YES

R LALIQUE

Is it marked "R Lalique", possibly with "France" and a model number?

NO — Sabino pieces are usually marked with a moulded engraved signature.

Opalescent figurine by Edmund Etling et Cie £1,000

YES

IF ALL THE ANSWERS ARE "YES" THEN YOU PROBABLY DO HAVE A HIGHLY DESIRABLE PIECE OF LALIQUE.

CERAMICS

Whether you prefer the subtle sensuality of the Art Nouveau potters, or the uncluttered modern approach of the Art Deco era, the pottery of the late 19th and early 20th centuries provides something to suit almost every taste. If you are an inexperienced collector interested in ceramics this could be an ideal choice of subject to begin with: there is a wide variety of designers and styles available; most pottery and porcelain is marked by the manufacturer; wares by the most famous potters are usually well documented;

and many pieces are still refreshingly inexpensive.

During the Art Nouveau period the surfaces of plates and vases were covered with floral and organic shapes, or the languid, scantily clad maidens, synonymous with the style of the movement. In stark contrast, the clean bright geometric motifs and dramatic avant-garde shapes which evolved in the Art Deco pottery of the 20s and 30s evoke equally effectively the optimistic and forward-looking spirit of their age.

◀ WILLIAM MOORCROFT

If you see a piece of pottery decorated with raised lines, which look as if they've been applied with an icing nozzle, the chances are it was made by William Moorcroft, at the famous Macintyre Pottery in Staffordshire. This "Iris" vase illustrates the distinctive technique, known as "tube-line" which was made with hand-applied fine lines of slip. £1,200

▶ DOULTON & CO

This factory produced such a wide variety of wares that many buyers collect nothing else! You'll have to pay more if a piece of Doulton was made by a famous designer. This vase was decorated by the prominent designer Mark V. Marshall, and would be worth over £5,000; a piece by a less prestigious designer might only be worth 10% of that price.

▲ ROYAL COPENHAGEN

The serpentine movement of this group, and the soft pastel shades with which it's decorated, identify this as a typical piece of Royal Copenhagen porcelain. The group, known as "The Rock and the Wave", is so popular that it's still reproduced today. Dating can be tricky but different marks were used and these can give a clue as to when the piece was made. £700–900

1894–1900   1894–1922   from 1905

CLARICE CLIFF

The most famous British Art Deco potter, Clarice Cliff, produced such a plethora of diverse shapes and designs that whole sales are now devoted entirely to her wares. Value is largely determined by the rarity of the design. Small objects, or anything in the "Crocus" pattern are usually the most affordable.

Although produced in large quantities, all genuine Clarice Cliff was hand-painted and you should be able to see brush strokes in the coloured enamels.

FUTURISTIC SHAPES

Exemplified by this unusual c.1935 teapot with its bizarrely curving lid, dramatic futuristic shapes are a keynote of Clarice Cliff's adventurous pottery.
£300–500

Condition is of paramount importance to value and restoration can be difficult to spot. Check spouts and handles for signs of chipping and run a finger around rims and bases to see if they're intact.

Most pieces are marked with a printed mark and a facsimile signature.

Decoration is often outlined in black.

The warm yellow "honey glaze" gives the background an ivory colour seen on many Clarice Cliff wares.

FAKES

Many reproductions and fakes of pieces by Clarice Cliff have appeared in the last decade. They can usually be distinguished by their inferior colour and design. Some fakes have photographically copied marks which usually have a fuzzy appearance. This jug looks washed out compared with the vibrant colours of the teapot, and the handle is too thin.

DESIRABLE DESIGNS
- Age of Jazz figures
- Wall masks
- *Inspiration* design pieces (now extremely rare)
- *Circus* series – designed by Dame Laura Knight
- Graham Sutherland designs
- Frank Brangwyn circular plaques.

SCULPTURE

Sculpture, which had hitherto been a rather expensive artistic medium, enjoyed an upsurge of popularity during the early 20th century, as new technology enabled founders to produce smaller scale models of monumental pieces. Inexpensive scaled-down figures epitomizing the Art Nouveau and Deco styles became widely available. One recurring subject is the female form; Art Nouveau sculpture shows women in dreamy poses, or draped across functional objects such as lamps. Sculpture from the Art Deco era is more stylized and reflects the dizzy Jazz Age, depicting elegant ladies dancing, playing golf and smoking.

◀ **GUSTAV GURSCHNER**
Form, function and decoration are typically intermingled in this bizarre *c.*1900 bronze nautilus shell lamb by Bavarian sculptor Gustav Gurschner. Similar fluid shapes were favoured by French sculptors; English pieces are usually less stylized. £3,000

▶ **FERDINAND PREISS**
The most valuable Art Deco sculptures are usually those made from "chryselephatine" – a combination of bronze and ivory. This one dates from the 1930s and was made by Ferdinand Preiss, one of the most famous sculptors of such figures. £4,000

▲ **DEMÈTRE CHIPARUS**
The bases of Art Deco sculptures are often integral to the composition and can provide a clue to the identity of the maker. The architectural quality of the base of this figure is typical of Chiparus. £9,000

BEWARE
Many less valuable Art Deco figures were made from patinated bronze – a bronze spelter (zinc alloy) base – combined with ivorene (simulated ivory usually made from plastic). To identify spelter scratch the metal underneath – a yellow colour means the piece is made from bronze; a silvery tone indicates spelter and means that the piece is far less valuable.

SCULPTURE CARE
The patination of a bronze is fundamental to its appeal. **Never** polish a bronze or you will seriously reduce its value.

POSTERS

The growth of the Art Nouveau movement coincided with the development of several increasingly versatile lithographic printing techniques. Prominent artists such as Jules Chéret (the father of the modern poster), Alphonse Mucha, and Adolphe J.M. Cassandre exploited the new media with unrivalled originality. Advertising posters were produced in prolific quantities and nowadays these are keenly collected. The designer, aesthetic appeal and condition of a poster all influence value.

PRINTING TECHNIQUES

ENGRAVING – copperplate incised with design, inked and printed.

ETCHING – copperplate coated with wax into which design is scratched, inked and printed.

LITHOGRAPH – design drawn on stone and fixed; different colour areas are treated with ink-resistant chemical, the stone is inked and printed.

PHOTOGRAVURE – image photographed, negative applied to a metal plate which is etched or engraved.

▼ALPHONSE MUCHA
Mucha's posters usually combine a romanticized female figure with elaborate decorative details such as flora and drapery. £3,000

IS IT OLD?
Art Nouveau and Art Deco posters have been much reproduced in recent years; reproductions are identifiable by:
- thicker, usually glossy, modern paper
- colour printing made up from tiny dots you can see with a magnifying glass – lithographs have flat areas of colour.
- a list of known fakes is available; contact the International Vintage Posters Dealers Association.

▲ JULES CHÉRET
Many original Art Nouveau posters were printed on cheap paper and have suffered from foxing, creasing, tearing, fading or staining. Avoid those that are badly damaged or glued onto a backboard. This Chéret poster is in unusually good condition. £900

▲ J.M. CASSANDRE
Art Deco style posters usually have simple but striking designs and focus on a single dominant image, with strong emphasis on lettering. This poster for the liner *Normandie* is the most valuable of the posters by the most famous poster designer of the period, the French artist Adolphe J.M. Cassandre. £6,000

Although many are too delicate to be used for their original purposes, you can often treat old textiles as you would a picture and hang them on your walls – and this is one reason why in recent years textiles have enjoyed a huge increase in popularity.

Because of their inherent fragility, age and condition are fundamental to the value of all antique textiles. Among the earliest and most valuable English needlework textiles are raised work pictures made in the 17th century. These embroidered pictures were padded to give a three-dimensional effect and often contain amazing inconsistencies of scale – figures may be dwarfed by gigantic insects, huge flowers loom over tiny houses – but this is all part of their naïve charm.

In America settlers made a wide variety of textiles using skills brought from Europe; crewelwork and canvas work from the colonies drew on European styles but enjoyed greater and more lasting popularity in the New World.

Textiles produced in the 19th century and early 20th century tend to be widely available and far less expensive. Those made in the Middle East, China, Japan and India are often especially colourful. European tapestries of this period often imitate earlier styles, but with a greater number of brighter colours. If a whole tapestry is beyond your budget you could buy a small fragment or a chair cover and make a cushion from it. There is also an abundance of samplers, shawls and lace from which to choose. These may vary in price from as little as £50 up to several thousand.

EMBROIDERY

Throughout the centuries sewing was an important pastime for ladies and children. Some multi-patterned embroideries served as a visual recipe book of different stitches. In general, the finer the stitching and the brighter the colours the more desirable the piece will be. Silk embroideries are usually more valuable than those sewn in wool. Because 19th century textiles are relatively abundant, it's best to avoid badly damaged pieces, unless they're particularly unusual.

▲ **RAISED WORK**
Raised work (also called stumpwork) is a style of embroidery which incorporates distinctive areas of raised decoration, formed by padding certain areas of the design. Even though this c.1660 picture has had some restoration done to the ivory silk background, it would still be worth £2,000–5,000.

SAMPLER CARE
As with any textile, samplers are vulnerable to fading, spotting and discoloration and should be hung away from strong sunlight and damp.

If you're storing them in a drawer, roll, rather than fold, the pieces to prevent damage from pressure and creasing. Also make sure they're well protected from moths – use plenty of mothballs.

▼ SUSANIS

According to local legends, embroidered Susanis (the word means stitch or needle in Persian), such as this one from Bokhara, were laboriously stitched by young girls before they were married. They were then used as a covering for the bridal bed and ripped in half when the bride lost her virginity! £1,000–3,000

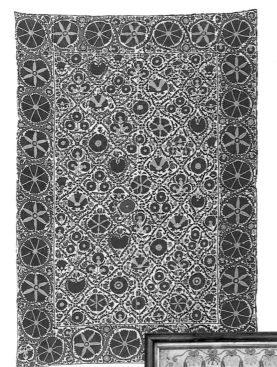

▲ BERLIN WOOLWORK

Berlin woolwork pictures, such as this, were made in large numbers in the mid-19th century. Subjects can vary enormously including everything from famous paintings to the royal family. This one shows a scene from a Sir Walter Scott novel and is worth about £200–500. Pictures of birds and dogs are always popular and can cost £600–1,000

► SAMPLERS

Early samplers were conceived as reference sheets showing various stitches and patterns, or as practice pieces. This sampler is worked in brightly coloured silks; typically it contains the name of the person who made it – Mary Read – and the date – 1838. £500–800

WHAT TO LOOK FOR

- Desirable subjects such as: houses, figures, alphabets, animals, birds, insects and flowers. Place names may also increase local interest and value.
- Samplers worked with wool rather than silk.
- Reasonable condition – avoid 19th century samplers if they're badly damaged or have holes. Those after 1850 tend to be less sought after.

WOVEN TEXTILES

In draughty 17th and 18th century interiors, tapestry hangings provided an essential source of warmth. It was only as wallpaper became popular, and houses were warmer, that tapestries dwindled in popularity. Nowadays, although no longer essential, tapestries have once again become collectable as fashionable home decorations. Not all are prohibitively expensive; you can find small snippets of flowery Aubusson, or finely woven Beauvais

◀ TAPESTRY
This 19th century Beauvais tapestry is so finely woven that you could easily mistake it for an oil painting – a sign that it's of the highest quality. The elaborate border is copied from picture frames of the period and the design is based on a painting by the 18th century artist François Boucher.
£5,000–8,000

◀ TAPESTRY CUSHIONS
Tapestry cushions are often fragments of a larger piece; this one uses 17th century tapestry which was probably once part of the border of a large panel. Like most cushions of this type, it's mounted on fabric of a much later date.
£400–600

LOOK FOR:
- rich, dark colours, especially red, orange, turquoise and gold.
- tightly woven, heavy, rich, soft woollen cloth enriched with silk.
- lots of individual colours (more colours means more complex weaving).
- complex designs inspired by Indian motifs
- large size – 272 x 145cm /107 x 57in is average, some measure over 381 x 192cm/150 x 76in.

▶ PAISLEY SHAWLS
Paisley shawls like this originally became popular because the voluminous crinoline skirts which were fashionable in the mid-19th century made it impossible for ladies to wear coats! Named after the town of Paisley in Scotland, they copied Kashmiri shawls but were mass-produced. Similar shawls were made in Edinburgh, Norwich and France. £300-400

tapestry for quite modest sums. Look out for door hangings (*portières*) and seat covers, or fragments of large tapestries, as these are often surprisingly inexpensive.

If the grandeur of a tapestry is too overpowering from your taste you might find the homely charm of an antique quilt or the delicacy of antique lace more appealing. The majority of quilts on the market date from the 19th and early 20th century and have become popular with collectors in Europe and America, where many of the finest were made. Some American examples bear the name of the maker and are considered folk art.

Most lace seen today dates from the latter half of the 19th century. Handmade lace has an appealing irregularity in its appearance, and early pieces, especially those dating from the 17th and 18th centuries, are particularly sought after by collectors.

▶ LOOKING AFTER LACE

- Early lace, such as this 18th century flounce, was usually made from linen, a robust fibre, so pieces can be framed and hung on a wall. £2,500
- Never display lace by pinning it – rust stains are extremely difficult to remove.
- Store lace between sheets of acid-free tissue paper.

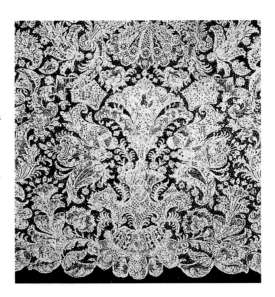

▼ DATING A QUILT

Newspaper or scrap paper templates were often used to stiffen the fabric patches in old quilts such as this American one. You might find laundry lists, letters, or news stories – and these can indicate the date and maker of the quilt. £1,000–3,000

Dolls are one of the most enduring types of toy. They have been played with and treasured by children both rich and poor from the earliest times to the present day. Most dolls are categorized by collectors according to the medium of the head (which is often different from that of the body). Among the most valuable dolls are carved wooden examples made in Britain in the 18th century and French dolls made from bisque during the 19th century; both types can fetch several thousand pounds at auction. But you don't have to spend a fortune to build up an interesting collection of dolls. Composition (a substance similar to *papier mâché*), wax over composition and fabric dolls are far less expensive.

Clothes may add to the value of any doll. Some had extremely elaborate wardrobes and those in their original costumes command a premium. Outfits and hairstyles which reflect the fashions at the time of production are particularly collectable. However, don't ignore badly dressed or even naked dolls. If your doll hasn't got a thing to wear, one way of boosting her value is to buy her a new outfit!

Teddy bears are a much newer type of toy and a relatively recent addition to the collector's market. The jointed bear was only invented at the turn of the 20th century, although soft toy animals did appear slightly earlier. The most sought-after bears are those made by Steiff, the premier maker of German bears. English bears from the 1930s and later tend to be more affordable, although equally appealing.

DOLL TYPES

During the 19th and 20th centuries many new doll-making techniques were developed. Media as varied as *papier mâché*, Parian, rag, celluloid, wax, plastic and vinyl were all experimented with and used to make dolls. Because the range of dolls available is so extensive, some enthusiasts choose to focus their collections on dolls made from one particular material. The table opposite highlights four different categories of doll; each has its own unique features which can help you identify similar pieces. By no means are all the dolls featured very old or priceless – as you will discover, even your old Barbie or Sindy can be collectable!

> **Bisque dolls** are the largest group of collector's dolls and are covered on the following two pages.

HEAD TYPES

Dolls are classified according to their head types; these illustrations show some of the most common types:

Shoulder head

Swivel head

Open head

Solid domed head

POURED WAX
A Madame Montinari
poured wax doll
£400–2,000

WAX OVER
COMPOSITION
A Pumpkin head doll
£100–300

FABRIC
A Lenci pressed felt
doll £1,800–2,000

VINYL
A pair of c.1960s
Barbies £100–400

IDENTIFYING FEATURES			
• hollow wax head and shoulders modelled in one piece • stiff muslin or fabric body • closed mouth • inserted eyes and hair • wax arms and legs	• large hollow moulded head made from *papier mâché* dipped in wax and painted • pupilless eyes • card, cloth or *papier mâché* body • turned wooden legs and arms	• moulded fabric head and stuffed fabric body • painted or stitched facial features • hair made from wood, cotton or mohair or painted on	• hollow soft vinyl head • rooted hair • jointed limbs • painted or inserted eyes • registered trademark on head or body
• dolls by famous makers, especially Pierotti, Montinari and John Edwards • softly modelled features • glass eyes • well-defined fingers and toes	• good condition – these dolls aren't rare so damage is not acceptable • real hair or moulded bonnets – rare but desirable • original, colourful, elaborate clothes	• dolls by famous makers such as Kathe Kruse, Lenci, Steiff • expressive features, sideways glancing eyes feature on Lenci • good condition – felt dolls are vulnerable to damage by moths • elaborate clothes with original labels	• Barbies with holes in the feet – these are the earliest • Barbies with titian or brunette hair • dolls from the 60s with designer-inspired wardrobes • dolls with original packaging • black Sindys

IDENTIFYING FEATURES

WHAT TO LOOK FOR

BISQUE DOLLS

Bisque dolls, whose heads are made from unglazed, tinted porcelain, are among the most elaborate and valuable of all collector's dolls. The first examples were produced by German makers in the 1850s, but the market was soon dominated by the French. The finest French bisques, made by leading makers such as Jumeau, Bru, Gaultier and Steiner, were expensive status symbols even when first made, and remained very much the province of pampered children from the most affluent homes. The earliest French bisques resembled fashionable ladies and came equipped with wardrobes of elaborate clothes, based on fashion plates of the day and are called fashion dolls. Later in the 19th century, the firm of Jumeau began making dolls with child-like features, large eyes and chubby bodies known as *bébés* – these soon became enormously popular, and although German manufacturers followed suit and produced their own child dolls they could never quite match the quality of the French *bébé*. German manufacturers eventually recovered the lion's share of the market in the early 20th century, when they introduced realistic "character" dolls, which had smiling crying, laughing and even frowning faces.

The price of bisque dolls ranges from thousands of pounds to a few hundred and is dependent on the maker, condition and quality, and on details such as the rarity of the mould number (the number on the back of the head which showed which mould was used) as well as the type of mouth (closed is best), eyes and body.

▼ GAULTIER FASHION DOLL

Fashion dolls can be dated by the shape of their bodies, which were made to fit the costumes of the day. This François Gaultier doll has a narrow waist and broad hips and shoulders well suited to her bustle dress – which was fashionable c.1870. £1,500–2,000

◀ JUMEAU DOLL

The *crème de la crème* of collector's dolls, Jumeaus, such as this *bébé*, are worth as much as £2,000–5,000. You can recognize a Jumeau by its pale-coloured bisque and large, glass eyes, usually blue. Early Jumeaus had numbers but no marks; later ones may have a red tick on their head.

Many bisque dolls have composition limbs and bodies which are prone to damage. Slight wear is acceptable and you should only repaint as a last resort.

GERMAN CHARACTER DOLLS

This bisque-headed doll was made by Ernst Heubach c.1914. It has an expressive face typical of German character dolls. She is of medium quality and would therefore be worth £200–500.

The value is reduced because the doll has a replacement wig – original wigs are always preferable.

This body is known as a "five piece bend limb" body, because the arms and legs are realistically bent.

Most bisque dolls have hand-painted eyebrows – delicately featured browns like this are a sign of quality.

Open mouths were introduced in c.1900. Although more expensive at the time, nowadays dolls with closed moths are more valuable than those with open ones.

GOOGLIE DOLLS

Some character dolls have very distinctive features and expressions. Dolls such as this, with roguish expressions, large round eyes and impish smiles, known as "Googlies", were inspired by the drawings of American illustrator Grace Debbie. They are among the most sought after types of character dolls. This one would be worth £2,000+.

This doll is wearing her original clothes which add to her value. If you need to replace your doll's clothes you can sometimes find old baby clothes to fit larger dolls, or use old fabric to make replacements. Always try to match new clothes to the doll's date.

TEDDY BEARS

Teddy bears have enjoyed a huge increase in popularity in recent years. The earliest bears were made by the Steiff company in Germany at the beginning of the 20th century. This well-known company was founded by Margaret Steiff who was crippled by polio and confined to a wheelchair as a child. With their pointed snouts, long arms and feet and humped backs, early Steiff bears look much more like real bears than most teddies of today, and are the most valuable of all collector's bears.

Bears are called "teddies" thanks to the American Ideal Toy Company. The company's founder, Morris Michtom, was inspired by a newspaper cartoon which showed President Theodore Roosevelt sparing the life of a grizzly bear. The cartoon was so popular that bears became adopted as the President's mascot, and Michtom reputedly wrote to ask his permission to call the bears he was making "Teddy". The President agreed and bears have been known as "Teddy" ever since.

As bears became more and more popular they were produced by increasing numbers of toy companies on both sides of the Atlantic. During World War I, and in the years that followed, British bear manufacturers expanded to fill the void left after German imports were banned. Prominent companies such as Chad Valley, Merrythought, Dean's Rag Book, Chiltern and J.K. Farnell enjoyed considerable success with their high-quality products.

Few bears were made during World War II, but after the war production resumed once more, although the appearance of bears subtly changed, becoming less realistic and more like the bears of today. Children's books and cartoons featuring bears also affected the market prompting reproductions of well-loved characters like Winnie-the-Pooh, Paddington, Sooty and Rupert Bear.

The most valuable bears for collectors are early examples, in good condition, made by famous makers. In general, Steiff bears remain the most valuable of because of their unique historical appeal and exceptionally high-quality workmanship.

BRITISH MAKERS

Several prominent British manufacturers of teddy bears prospered from c.1915 onwards. Most British bears were originally marked on fabric labels stitched to the foot:

◀ CHAD VALLEY
Chad bears date from the 1920s. Early bears were made of luxuriant mohair, usually gold coloured, with soft kapok stuffed limbs. £200–500

▶ MERRYTHOUGHT
Bears were made from the 1930s; this one has large round ears and joined claws which are typical of this maker. £300–900

▼ J.K. FARNELL & CO.
Farnell supplied teddy bears to Harrods during the 1920s. Winnie-the-Pooh was reputedly made by this company. The angled ears and large amber glass eyes of this c.1918 bear are typical of this maker. £1,500–3,000

STEIFF BEARS

This c.1908 bear is a good example of the most commonly seen type of Steiff bear. The humped back is typical of early Steiffs, as are the close-set eyes and round, widely spaced, ears. Later bears can be recognized by their less prominent humps.
£1,000–5,000

The earliest bears had black shoebutton eyes; glass eyes were only used after World War I. The eyes were attached by wires which can become loose; old bears should therefore not be left within reach of young children.

◀ MARKS
Steiff bears were marked in the ear with a distinctive button. Early buttons had an elephant logo or were plain. Later buttons had the word "Steiff" written on them.

The long curved limbs and large oval felt paws with narrow wrists and ankles are characteristic of Steiff bears.

BEAR CARE
- Holes can be mended without reducing value but use similar fabric for patches.
- Dirty bears need specialist cleaning; untreated dirt makes the fabric rot.
  - Put new additions in a plastic bag with mothballs over night to kill any infestation.

Paw pads are usually made from felt and are especially prone to wear; this bear has replacement pads, which will affect its value.

Most bears are made from beige or gold mohair plush. Unusual colours are more desirable. Steiff also made bears using red, apricot and white mohair, and even a few, sought-after, black bears.

AMERICAN BEARS
American bears, like this, were often unmarked but have distinctive wide barrel-shaped bodies, narrow arms and legs and small feet. Some have humps like German bears. £250+

The appeal of collecting old and antique toys and games seems to lie largely in the sense of nostalgia for earlier technologies, lifestyles – and a childhood past – which they evoke.

If you are thinking of beginning a collection of toys it is important to remember that there is a huge range of varieties and prices from which to choose. Many collectors specialize in one particular area, such as clockwork toys, robots or cars, or in a particular maker. You need to be sure of your area of interest before visiting the larger auction houses because many sell different types of toy – such as soldiers, model cars or trains – in specialist sales.

Prices for toys depend on the maker, the rarity of the model and the condition. Although chips and dents are virtually inevitable and therefore acceptable, a toy in mint condition, or with its original packaging is what every serious collector longs for. Repainting will nearly always reduce the value of a collector's toy so only repaint items in your collection as a last resort.

Toys made by well-known firms are always sought after, and minor damage is acceptable if the toy is made by a premium firm such as Bing, Märklin or Lehmann.

Viewing sales and visiting specialist dealers is the best way of getting to know which models are the most desirable. But once you have got a good feel for prices, you don't have to buy from an upmarket auction house or dealer. Because many collectable toys are not very old it's always worth scouring the local junk shop or jumble sale for bargains!

WOOD, LEAD & DIE-CAST TOYS

Less sophisticated than toys made from other substances, carved wooden toys have an appealing naivety. Wooden toys were produced in quantity by German makers during the 18th and 19th centuries and some very collectable wooden toys were also made in America by the Schoenhut Co.

Lead became popular as a medium for various types of soldiers and other toys during the late 19th century. In Germany, France and Britain high-quality solid and hollow-cast lead soldiers were produced by firms such as Lucotte, Heyde and William Britain and today these are among the most valuable of all toy soldiers.

Die-cast toys were also made by hollow casting and were first produced in France in *c*.1910. In Britain, Dinky Toys, part of the Meccano Co., dominated the market for die-cast toys from the 1930s–60s and rare Dinky advertisement vans or unusual series are well worth looking for. In the 1950s Mettoy's Corgi range began to grow, dominating the market by the 1960s and 70s.

DIE-CAST TOYS
Complete sets of die-cast toys are always desirable, especially when they come with the original packaging. Although this *c*.1937 box is battered it still adds a third to the value of the set of aeroplanes. £600–800

▶ WOODEN TOYS

Noah's Ark was a popular subject for German wooden toy-carvers. Value depends on size, quality and the number of animals. They sell very well, with prices going up to £6,000 in some cases. This 19th century one is large (69cm/27in wide), fairly elaborate and contains over 200 animals, so it would be worth £2,000–3,000; smaller, less elaborate arks cost from £200.

▼ VALUE

Many 20th century wooden toys are still affordably priced. This 1930s apple filled with skittles is worth about £20–25.

▼ TOY SOLDIERS

British toy soldiers are among the most sought-after collectors' soldiers. Many were made using the hollow-casting method. This particular set is very rare, because it is a special order paint finish of Indian Lancers, and includes a European officer. £2,000–3,000

TINPLATE, TRAINS & CELLULOID

Horse-drawn carriages, boats, submarines, cars and even airships are just some of the plethora of tinplate toys made in the late 19th and early 20th centuries which reflect contemporary developments in transport. German toy companies led the field in the manufacture of tinplate toys and those made by well-known firms such as Bing, Märklin and Lehmann are famed for their accuracy and quality. Trains were one of the most important forms of transport from the mid-19th century and not surprisingly trains provided toy-makers with a fertile source of inspiration and have since become one of the most sought-after type of collectable toy. The earliest 1830s toy trains were designed to be pulled along the floor

▶ **BING**
This *c*.1906 Bing rear-entry Tonneau with a clockwork mechanism is especially desirable because the high-quality hand-enamelled paintwork is in near perfect condition.
£6,000–8,000

◀ **MÄRKLIN**
Märklin toys, such as this spirit-fired torpedo boat, can be identified by their distinctive maker's mark, which in this case is stamped on the boat's rudder.
£5,500–6,500

▲ **TRAINS**
The most valuable toys, made between 1895 and 1914, are now well outside the price range of the average schoolboy. Märklin were the first company to use a numerical gauge system to identify the different sizes available. This Gauge III engine, made *c*.1909, is in the second largest size and would be worth £20,000+.

or steam powered, but by the 1850s–60s clockwork versions appeared. Eventually *c*.1890/1900 electric trains – the dream of every schoolboy ever since – began to be produced in substantial numbers.

With the beginning of the space race and the advent of science-fiction films like *The Forbidden Planet*, tinplate robots and space toys became popular. Rare examples of these early robot toys can make £10,000–20,000.

Celluloid toys were made from the late 19th century until the substance was made obsolete with the advent of plastics in the 20th century. These days celluloid toys are keenly collected although they are generally less expensive than tinplate toys of a similar date.

DISNEY TOYS

The earliest toys representing Disney characters were produced by German toy manufacturers such as Distler, who was probably responsible for this 1930s clockwork Mickey Mouse barrel organ toy. This thin, rather gloomy-looking Mickey is the most valuable. Even though he's lost his tail, Minnie has been repainted, and there are signs of rusting, the piece would still be worth over £2,500.

WHAT TO LOOK FOR
- Mickey and Minnie on a motorcycle, by Tipp & Co – a boxed version recently sold for a record £51,000.
- Mickey the Musical Mouse, by Nifty
- Mickey the Drummer, by Nifty
- Donald Ducks with long bills.

◀ **LICENSING**
The box of this celluloid Mickey riding Pluto, produced in Japan for the Western market, shows that it was made under special licence and is therefore more desirable than an unauthorized version.
£2,000–3,000

CELLULOID
Toys made from celluloid are highly flammable and prone to denting and cracking. The substance is almost impossible to restore satisfactorily, so avoid damaged celluloid toys.

Memorabilia associated with the popular music industry of the 20th century is one of the newest, most exciting and often accessibly priced collecting areas – although it does have its high prices too – the current record being the $2.3 million paid for John Lennon's Rolls-Royce in 1985.

Almost any object in some way connected with a well-known star can be collectable, so even tickets, posters and other printed ephemera made for concerts and tours are saleable. The most sought-after pieces are those closely linked with the stars themselves. Collectors pay especially high prices for the musical instruments with which a star is associated; electric guitars can fetch many thousands of pounds if they were played at a memorable concert. The Fender Stratocaster, played by Jimi Hendrix at Woodstock in 1969, was sold in 1990 for £198,000.

Clothes are another popular collecting area. The most valuable garments are those recognizably linked with the image of their owner. Perhaps they were photographed wearing them, or used them at an important concert, or in a video. Elton John's wacky platform shoes, Madonna's gold leather Jean-Paul Gaultier corset and Michael Jackson's rhinestone-studded glove have all received huge media attention and have attracted prices to match whenever they've come under the hammer. But not all collectable clothes are prohibitively expensive – prices for a roadie's jacket, or a souvenir T-shirt sporting the name and logo of a tour or album start at less than £100.

THE 50s & 60s

The golden era of rock 'n' roll is not surprisingly the focus for many collectors' attentions. Memorabilia from this period is relatively scarce compared with that of the following decades, so even printed concert programmes and magazines, which were made in their thousands, and once cost only a few shillings, are keenly collected. The most desirable memorabilia relates to the big names of the period whose popularity endures today. Among the most popular are Elvis Presley, Buddy Holly, Bill Haley and Bob Dylan – to name but a few.

▲ **BUDDY HOLLY**
Buddy Holly still has a keen following and memorabilia relating to his career attracts high prices. This signed souvenir programme from 1958 marks his group's only tour in Britain. £600–800

▲ **JIM MORRISON**
Jim Morrison, the lead singer of the Doors, has always been collectable but his popularity enjoyed an upsurge after the release of Oliver Stone's film charting his life. These working lyrics for the song *The Celebration of the Lizard* provide a revealing glimpse into Morrison's creative processes and are worth £5,000+.

BEATLES MEMORABILIA

The Beatles have a unique place in the history of pop music: no previous group had enjoyed such enormous and lasting success and they pioneered the vibrant new pop music which epitomized the sounds of the 1960s. Just as they dominated the charts, so they are clearly still 'No 1' to collectors of pop memorabilia, a position unchallenged since regular auctions of associated material began in the early 1980s. In fact almost any object associated with the group is of interest to collectors.

▲ BEATLES DOLLS
The wide range of Beatles merchandise made during the 1960s and 70s reflects the group's phenomenal popularity. Among the diverse Beatles objects which come up for sale are furnishings, jewellery, clothing, games, books, wigs and even confectionry. These Beatles dolls, dressed in Sgt. Pepper's Lonely Hearts Club Band costumes are worth £100–200.

▶ LENNON DRAWINGS
This hand-drawn Christmas card (above) was given to Cynthia Powell by John Lennon in 1958 and encloses a revealing eight-page letter to Cynthia, whom he married five years later. Drawings by John Lennon, who also wrote and illustrated two books, are among the most desirable Beatles memorabilia and can fetch very high prices. £10,000+

▶ RINGO DRUM SET
Although this drum set is only a toy it would still attract collectors because it is rare to find one in near-perfect condition; this one comes complete with sticks, stand, original box and instructions. £250–400

WHAT TO LOOK FOR
- Handwritten lyrics to famous songs
- Autographed and handwritten letters
- Autographed photographs – often faked, so beware
- Artwork for record sleeves
- Animation cells from *Yellow Submarine*

THE 70s

The 70s marked the heyday of rock star rebels like Led Zeppelin, David Bowie, Marc Bolan, Bruce Springsteen, Iggy Pop, The Ramones and The Sex Pistols. These artists had a new approach to rock music, based around live performances and album sales, which was to have a profound influence on musicians of the following generations.

As supplies of 1960s memorabilia diminish, it is likely that collectors will turn increasingly to the 70s and that memorabilia from this decade will to become increasingly desirable.

▼ PETE TOWNSHEND
The fact that this guitar has been smashed to bits paradoxically adds to its value because it highlights its original owner's "bad boy" image. It was sold accompanied by a letter which details the guitar's history: *"…I broke it in 1973 in a rage of frustration in my studio …"* £4,000–5,000

▲ THE ISLE OF WIGHT FESTIVAL
Posters relating to important concerts are among the more affordable pieces of rock and pop memorabilia. The pop festivals held in the Isle of Wight in 1969 and 1970 were key events and attracted audiences of over a quarter of a million. This colourful promotional poster, advertising the 1970 concert, is worth £60–100.

◀ ELTON JOHN
Elton John is one star who has pushed the possibilities of stage costume to its limits. Extraordinary glasses and eccentric hats, brightly coloured suits and flamboyant shoes such as these became his trademarks and are keenly collected. £400–800 (a pair)

THE 80s & 90s

The advent of the pop video and the growing importance of television in the music industry was largely responsible for the increased emphasis stars of the 1980s and 90s have attached to their appearance and image. As concerts and tours became increasingly sophisticated, the star's visual impact became as important as the music. Costumes, often made by leading fashion designers, are an obvious way of establishing the star's persona. Unsurprisingly then, outfits of increasingly extravagant design have become the symbol of some of the most famous celebrities of the past two decades.

▶ PRINCE

The clothes of the Artist Formerly Known As Prince are specially made for him and, because his colourful, swashbuckling outfits are fundamental to his on-stage image, those that come up for sale are very desirable. This suit made from turquoise and blue silk was sold with a letter of authentication stating where it was made and confirming that it was worn at the 1988 Grammy Awards by the artist. £5,000+

TOP FIVE COLLECTABLE STARS

- **Michael Jackson** Leading light so almost anything is desirable.
- **Madonna** Changes her image for each tour so anything directly connected with one of her "looks" will be very desirable.
- **Prince** Neo-romantic clothes always sought after.
- **Elton John** Shoes, glasses, hats – the more zany the higher the price.
- **Queen** Anything connected with Freddie Mercury.

PRESENTATION DISCS

Among the most valuable awards presented to the star are the "gold" and "platinum" discs celebrating record sales. In the United States gold discs are given for over 500,000 albums, or 1 million singles sold; platinum discs are given for over 1 million albums or 2 million singles sold. This U.K. silver presentation disc for Madonna's *You Can Dance* is worth £300–400.

▲ MICHAEL JACKSON

Michael Jackson was often photographed wearing this rhinestone-studded glove which was perhaps the most instantly recognizable piece of rock and pop clothing of the decade. The glove was sold in 1991 for £16,500; a record for any piece of Michael Jackson costume!

Whether because of their historical interest, high-quality craftsmanship, or because they are such potent reminders of the heroics of the past, the relics of war have long fascinated collectors. The terms "Arms and Militaria" cover a suprisingly wide range of objects and include armour, firearms, edged weapons, medals, badges, uniforms, and even prints and cigarette cards.

Armour has been made, in one form or another, from the dawn of civilization to the 19th century but most pieces commonly seen on the market today date from the 16th century onwards. Full sets of armour are rare and extremely valuable, the majority are incomplete and if you're a novice collector you must learn to recognize the numerous "marriages" between pieces from different periods. So long as you realize the set is a composite and this fact is allowed for in the price, marriages are acceptable.

Antique firearms are often the most accessibly priced items in this field. A 19th century flintlock pistol could cost £150 or less; 18th century examples are priced from about £300. Arms and militaria tend to be collected by people with a deep interest in the subject, rather than speculators and investors, and as a result prices for all categories of militaria tend to show steady sustained growth rather than the wild fluctuations caused by changing fashions. Before you start buying, remember to check if a special licence is necessary. In most countries you don't need a licence to collect antique firearms, but you do if you intend firing them.

EDGED WEAPONS & FIREARMS

Edged weapons, which include swords, sabres, dirks and bayonets, come up for sale frequently and, depending on the type of weapon you choose, it is possible to build up a collection for relatively little outlay. Most antique firearms fall into one of two categories: flintlocks, which use a flint to make a spark and ignite the charge; or percussion guns, in which a metal cap containing a small explosive charge is ignited by the stroke of the hammer. Even though most antique weapons are never used, the "feel" of a firearm is one of the most important factors to take into account when buying. Firearms should be well balanced when you handle them. Pieces which feel top-heavy and uncomfortable in the firing position are less desirable.

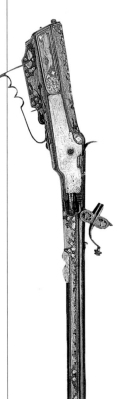

◄ LONG ARMS
Unusual early weapons always command a premium. This German wheel-lock sporting rifle, dated 1666, has several quality features which make it particularly desirable:
- high-quality engraving on the lock plate
- maker's mark
- elaborately inlaid stock decorated with stag horn, silver wire and mother-of-pearl. £3,000–5,000

SWORD CARE
- wipe blades clean after handling
- wax blades after cleaning
- clean rust spots by rubbing them with a copper coin.

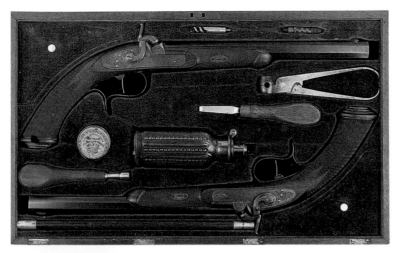

◀ DUELLING PISTOLS

In cased sets of pistols always check that all the pieces belong together and have not been added. This pair of American percussion duelling pistols comes with a range of accessories including balls and Eley caps.
£2,000–3,000

◀ SWORDS AND DIRKS

The less than perfect condition and evidence of honest wear you can see on this set of mid-19th century Scottish regimental swords are a good sign that the set is authentic. It is also unusual to find such an set in its own case.
£3,500–5,500

- The small dagger in the centre is a Scottish dirk; these were carried by Scottish Highlanders.

BEWARE

- Fake engraving is sometimes added to swords to increase their value – be suspicious of harsh bright edges, and expect there to be signs of ageing, such as dirt and grease between the lines.
- When fake engraving is added to a piece which already has some decoration it will often be of a different depth from the original and the background colour will be different.

▼ DECORATION

The decoration on a sword usually reflects the status of its original owner and always adds to value. The blued and inlaid Napoleonic sabre (top) once belonged to a high-ranking cavalry officer. The 1831 British general officer's sword (below) is less ornate, reflecting the owner's lower rank.
top £800–1,200
below £300–400

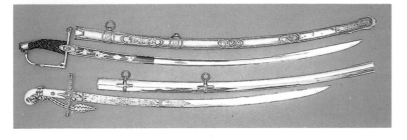

ARMOUR

Antique armour of all periods is highly collectable; swashbuckling armour from the English Civil War (1642–49) is in fact still fought over, but nowadays by collectors! Among the most sought-after items of this period are "lobster-tailed" cavalry helmets, pikeman's pots (simple helmets), breastplates, backplates and gauntlets. Because complete suits of original armour so rarely come up for sale, even good 19th century reproductions are highly collectable and valuable. Much good-quality armour of this period was made in Germany, France and Spain.

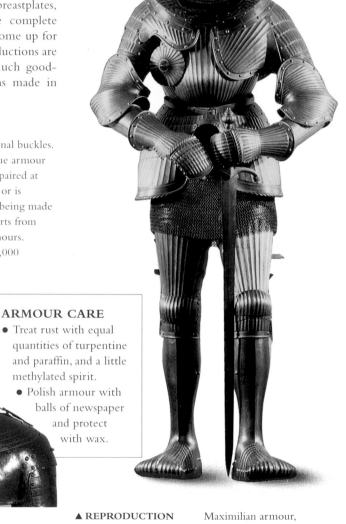

▼ CONDITION

This three-quarter armour dates from c.1640 and was made for a cuirassier (horseman). It is in unusually fine condition and even has its original buckles. Most antique armour has been repaired at some stage, or is composite, being made up using parts from various armours.
£8,000–12,000

ARMOUR CARE
- Treat rust with equal quantities of turpentine and paraffin, and a little methylated spirit.
- Polish armour with balls of newspaper and protect with wax.

WHAT TO LOOK FOR
- Armourer's marks – add to value.
- Small dents in the breast plate – made from a pistol ball fired to test the armour's strength – a good sign of age.
- Funerary helmets – worn at funerals.

▲ REPRODUCTION ARMOUR

Although 19th century armour was intended for decorative purposes, much of it was very well made. The quality of this 16th century-style fluted Maximilian armour, made c.1820 (possibly by Wincklemeyer of Vienna), is reflected in the thickness of the metal used. A good-quality suit will weigh 26–27kg (58–60lb).
£8,000–10,000

MISCELLANEOUS MILITARIA

The wide range of other collectable military antiques provides would-be collectors with huge scope. You may decide to concentrate on a particular regiment, a type of object, or on a period of military history. Complete early uniforms may be hard to find, but head-dresses, badges, fastenings, medals, powder flasks, postcards and prints are readily available and can form fascinating and highly decorative collections.

▶ **BADGES**

Whether made from metal or fabric badges are increasingly popular with collectors. Officer's headdress badges are larger than most others and particularly sought after. British regimental badges such as these early 19th century examples are identifiable because they invariably include a crown in the design.
£300–400 (each)

▲ **SHAKOS**

Shakos, the cylindrical helmets, with peaks and often plumes, were popular during the 19th century. The elaborateness of their decoration can affect value. This Austro-Hungarian shako is in reasonable condition and is decorated with ornate gold trimming. It is therefore worth around £300–500.

BEWARE
- Expect badges to show evidence of their age – those in perfect condition should make you suspicious.
- Fake badges usually weigh less than genuine ones and feel waxy.

▶ **MEDALS**

Before buying a medal check the soldier's and regiment's history to make sure he was entitled to it. This rare group of medals, awarded to a colonel in the Indian Army, is officially engraved with his name.
£2,500–3,000

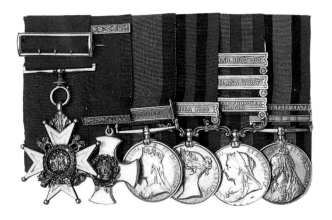

SCIENTIFIC INSTRUMENTS

However tempting it is to imagine some famous scientist of the past making a dramatic discovery with your microscope, sadly this is usually a long way from the truth. Most early scientific instruments were made either for amateur scientists, who regarded them as objects of beauty, or for professionals like surveyors, navigators, architects and even teachers, for whom these were everyday tools of their trade.

You don't have to be knowledgeable about the history of science to appreciate the obvious skill with which scientific instruments were made. At one end of the spectrum are the machine-made precision tools produced during the 19th century, some of which can be bought for little over £100 (even though

BEWARE
During the early 19th century unscrupulous dealers attempted to cash in on the Dollond reputation by selling telescopes falsely inscribed Dolland. These are still collectable but less valuable.

◀ TELESCOPES
John Dollond perfected the use of achromatic lenses, which eliminated the problems of colour fringing (caused by the distortion of light) in telescopes. Instruments made by this leading 18th century London maker or his sons, Peter and John jnr, are often signed "*J.*" or "*P. Dollond London*". This one dates from the late 18th century and is worth £2,500–3,500.

▶ SEXTANTS AND OCTANTS
Octants (so-called because their frame is one-eighth of a circle) and sextants (one-sixth) measure angular distance using reflective mirrors. Octants usually have wooden frames – mahogany, ebony or boxwood are typical. Sextants were usually brass-framed, were more accurate than octants and are often more expensive. This is an 18th century brass and ebony octant signed by J. MacDonald. £400–600

they may originally have cost as much as a small house!); at the other there are the rare, expensive examples of 18th century hand-crafted objects which are always in demand and important Renaissance instruments which have come to be regarded as works of art in their own right and also command very high prices. Many instruments are also ornately decorated and incorporate materials such as brass, silver, ivory and ebony. The dating of a piece can present inexperienced collectors with problems, as the same design was often repeated over long periods. Some instruments were marked by their maker, and this usually helps with identification and dating, but also will usually increase the price. Fakes and reproductions of early instruments exist, so if in doubt always consult an expert.

> **NEVER...**attempt to polish an old scientific instrument of any type without checking with an expert first. If you do so you may seriously damage its patina, and reduce its value dramatically.

▲ GLOBES

Terrestrial pocket globes like this reflect advances in mapping and circumnavigation of the world and often had cases lined with celestial globes – maps of the stars. This one was made by J. Smith in 1815.
£2,000–3,000

▼ MICROSCOPES

This Culpeper-type microscope dates from *c*.1730 and is one of the most desirable types of early microscope. It is worth £5,000–8,000. Microscopes from the 19th century are easier to find. Quality makers to look out for are: Powell & Lealand, W. & S. Jones, James Powell Swift, Smith & Beck, Nachet & Sons, Carl Zeiss and Secretan.

◄ SUNDIALS

Before watches became widely accessible and reliable, sundials were often used to check the time. There are two main types of dial: the pedestal dial, most commonly used in the garden, and the pocket dial, designed to be used at any latitude. This 18th century octagonal pocket dial has an elaborately decorated brass plate and a folding gnomon (the part that casts the shadow). £300–400

CAMERAS & PHOTOGRAPHS

Although old cameras seem worlds apart from the high-tech models of today, many are still in working order and are bought to use. The earliest commercially manufactured cameras were produced from *c.*1841 and used the daguerreotype process, developed in France by L.J.M. Daguerre in 1837. However, each daguerreotype image was unique and it was not until Henry Fox Talbot's invention of the calotype that multicopies could be produced from a single exposure. Among the most intriguing of cameras are the novelty, detective and spy cameras which began to be produced as the photographic process became more refined towards the end of the century.

Unlike many other collectables, a camera's age is not necessarily reflected in its value – the rarity and quality of a particular model are often far more important than when it was made. Japanese cameras, which have enjoyed an upsurge in popularity recently, were mass-produced in the aftermath of World War II. Their quality became widely appreciated as a result of photojournalists covering the Korean War who recognized the superior quality of Japanese lenses. Today, rare and limited edition models by companies such as Nikon or Canon can fetch very high prices.

▶ **DAGUERREOTYPES**

Daguerreotypes look like mirrors – the image is formed on silvered metal, usually protected behind sealed glass. Despite their relative rarity you can still find portrait groups such as this for £60–100. An interesting view or a known sitter adds to value, which can be £1,000 or more.

◀ **PHOTOGRAPH ALBUMS**

The value of early photo albums is largely determined by the subject matter of the photos and the quality of the album. This one is made from leather and mother-of-pearl. Some were made of ivory, silver, gold or mauchline ware – wood covered with tartan-printed paper. £150–200

WHAT TO LOOK FOR

- milestone cameras which incorporate unusual technical innovations
- early handmade brass and mahogany cameras
- unusual spy cameras
- rare models by Ernst Leitz (Leica) and Zeiss
- limited edition post-World War II Japanese cameras.

► DETECTIVE AND SPY CAMERAS

Cameras in the form of books, watches, rings and packets of cigarettes may have been made more as curiosities than for any real espionage or skulduggery, but are nonetheless highly popular with today's collectors – and can fetch very high prices. This *c*.1895 camera looks just like a pocket watch when closed and measures only 4cm (1¾in) diameter. Made in America by John C.

Hegelein, it's one of only three examples known at present. £15,000–20,000.

▲ WOODEN, BRASS AND MAHOGANY CAMERAS

Although prices for wooden cameras start from around £200, early mahogany and brass-bound cameras are always sought after, but this 1890 Cyclographe is especially rare because it is the first panoramic camera produced by the prominent French maker V. Damoizeau. A clockwork mechanism rotated the camera around the platform and wound on the film automatically. £8,000–12,000

► JAPANESE CAMERAS

The quality and condition of post-war cameras has important effects on their price. This Nikon S3M is one of only 195 models made in the series, comes with an S72 motor and is in near-mint condition. It would be worth about £25,000–35,000. A similar used model would cost £15,000.

FILM MEMORABILIA

Although there is nothing new about the magnetic allure of the silver screen, film memorabilia is one of the most recent and exciting arrivals on the collecting scene. All the glamour of the movies, from the nostalgic old films of Hollywood's golden age to the high-tech special effects films of the 1980s and 90s, are reflected in the objects which fall into this colourful collecting category.

The major types of collectable film memorabilia are costumes, props, autographs, posters and photographs; but almost anything associated with a particular film or star can be collectable. Props associated with the key stars of cult movies tend to attract the highest prices. If a particular object immediately conjures up an important star you're on to a winner – but you will probably have to pay for it! If you can't afford the thousands neccessary to buy objects such as Charlie Chaplin's bowler hat and cane, or Harrison Ford's whip, you can still join in the fun by collecting the more affordable types of film memorabilia available. Posters, photographs, autographs and publicity stills are often priced at less than £100.

▶ **PHOTOGRAPHS**
This portrait photograph of Marlene Dietrich dates from c.1935, but even recently reproduced photos are desirable, because to many collectors a classic image of the star is more important than the age of the photograph. £300–550

BEWARE
Autographs on photos are often not genuine:
● Many stars allowed their secretaries to sign photographs on their behalf.
● Sometimes the negative of the photograph was signed.
● Some photographs are stamped with the star's signature.

◀ **POSTERS**
Among the most desirable film posters are those from classic films of the 50s and 60s. *Breakfast at Tiffany's,* for example, met with enormous success when it was released in 1961, and firmly established Audrey Hepburn as a star of the first order. This poster fetched £400. Posters for lesser films can still be found for under £20.

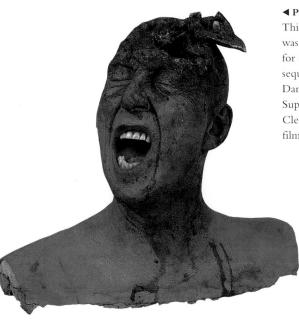

◀ PROPS

This gruesome head was used in *Aliens 3* for close-up sequences of Charles Dance, who played Superintendent Clemens in the 1992 film. Its high value is a reflection of three key points:

● rarity – it was the only one made
● the character was a key one in the film
● The *Alien* films were, and still are, hugely popular. £2,000+

▼ THUNDERBIRDS

The demand for Thunderbirds memorabilia has been fuelled by the various re-runs of the series on TV. Even though this is only a replica of Thunderbird 3, and wasn't used in filming, it's still worth £600–800.

▲ STAR WARS

The best film props are surprisingly well made and sophisticated. Darth Vader's helmet is made from fibreglass and has see-through perspex panels inserted in the cheek and neck areas to give better visibility to the wearer during the fighting sequences of *Star Wars*. £3,000+

▶ CLAPPERBOARDS

Clapperboards are among the least expensive types of film memorabilia. Look for boards which come from popular films, and which are printed with the name of the production and the director. £50+

SPORTING COLLECTABLES

If your attic is filled with mouldering old golf clubs you may be astonished to know that less than a decade ago an antique club fetched £92,400 at auction! While such a staggering price is very much the exception, there are, nonetheless, increasing numbers of sportsmen who bring their passion for field, pitch, or river bank into their homes by collecting objects related to their favoured pastime. Prices have also been boosted by the fashion for traditional décor which has inspired many an interior designer to furnish elegant hallways and studies with the paraphernalia of a time-honoured sport.

In the not too distant past old sporting equipment was usually relegated to the junk shop; nowadays you're more likely to find it in upmarket auction houses, and there are also a number of dealers who specialize in this field.

The most sought-after sporting items relate to the most popular pastimes: hence golf, fishing, football, tennis, cricket, rugby and even skiing memorabilia are keenly collected by enthusiasts. Spectator sports are also popular: for example, horse racing, Formula 1, boxing, the Olympic Games, and in the United States there is, of course, baseball. Collectable items include not only the objects needed to pursue the sport – whether rods, reels, golf clubs, balls or rackets – but also trophies of the sport and ceramic and printed ephemera relating to it.

◄ GOLF
Pre-19th century golfing collectables are extremely rare, which explains why this late 17th–early 18th century club made by a blacksmith reached the world record price of £92,400 when it was sold at auction.

WHAT TO LOOK FOR
- Clubs marked by one of the great makers such as Auchterlonie, Andrew Forgan, Jack Morris or Philp.
- Feathery golf balls – made from hand-stitched leather stuffed with dampened goose down.
- Pottery commemorating golfing events or personalities, especially if made by premier British factories such as Spode and Doulton.

▲ 19TH CENTURY CLUBS
Early hand-crafted clubs had names rather than numbers. These are drivers and long-nosed spoons of varying sizes. Before c.1850 clubs had long, slender heads, but by the 1880s the head had become shorter with a thicker neck. Value depends on rarity, age, quality and condition. Wood and iron clubs were made until the 1930s and can still be bought for £20–30. These clubs date from c.1885 and range from £1,500 to £3,500.

◀ **FISHING**

Perhaps as a substitute for "the one that got away", fishing trophies of the late 19th–early 20th century have lured many a collector in recent years. The most desirable fish are those in bow-fronted cases, such as this, which contains a bream caught in 1935.
£700–900

▲ **FISHING TACKLE**

Early reels were finely made from materials such as brass, ivorene (an ivory substitute) and ebonite (simulated ebony); examples with maker's marks are particularly desirable. Among the names to look out for are Hardy Bros of Alnwick, Charles Farlow, S. Allcock and Alfred Illingworth. These reels all date from the late 19th and early 20th centuries and are worth between £150 (top right) and £2,000 (bottom right).

CONDITION

Reels in mint condition are rare, but those with damaged or replaced parts, or which have their owner's name scratched on them (unless he is famous) are best avoided.

▼ **TENNIS**

Even if he or she never won a match with it, a famous owner can transform a racket into a collector's item. When the racket Fred Perry used to beat Jack Crawford at Wimbledon in 1934 was auctioned, it sold for £23,000. This Wilson racket is autographed by Jimmy Connors, who used it in the 1979–81 US Opens, and comes with a letter of authenticity.
£1,500–2,000

BOXES

Decorative boxes come in a huge range of shapes, sizes and prices; some of the most exquisite ones were produced during the 18th century to contain snuff, patches or tobacco. The highest-quality boxes were often made from gold or silver, perhaps decorated with precious stones, but others were made from less expensive metals. Enamelled and porcelain boxes were also popular, some of the most attractive being made in the shape of a bird or animal. Boxes have long been fashionable items to collect and small 18th century boxes can easily cost £1,000 or more, but you can still find attractive 19th century versions for much less. Price is usually determined by quality and the type of materials used. In general, boxes made from wood or *papier mâché* are more widely available and affordable.

▲ LACQUER BOXES
Lids of 19th century lacquer boxes were often decorated with a copy of a well-known Old Master – erotic subjects were always especially popular. This one shows nymphs bathing, with mischievous voyeurs in the bulrushes. Like many boxes of this type it was made in Germany, and is stamped on the interior "*Stobwasser Fabrik*". £500–800

▼ ENAMEL BOXES
Bilston (Staffordshire), Birmingham and Battersea led the field in producing English enamel boxes during the 18th century. Chipping will reduce value; this late 18th century box is damaged around the base and is worth £150–200; a similar case in better condition might well cost twice as much.

▲ TORTOISESHELL BOXES
Tortoiseshell, moulded by heat and pressure, was often used for making small boxes during the 18th and 19th centuries. This 19th century cigar case is decorated with stellar *piqué* (an inlay of gold or silver). £200–300

◀ TUNBRIDGE WARE
Tunbridge decoration was mostly made, as the name suggests, in the Tunbridge Wells area of Kent. This fiddly technique involved making pictures from long strands of differently coloured woods which were glued together, and sliced transversally into thin sheets. Value depends on the fineness of the decoration; this one is of average quality. £400–500

VINTAGE FOUNTAIN PENS

Condition is a prime factor in the value of old pens, as they can be expensive to restore, so check carefully for signs of excessive wear. Avoid pens with replacement parts, which have often been forced or glued to the body. . Pens in excellent condition are worth four or five times as much as worn ones. Specially designed large and oversized pens are also well worth looking out for.

PREMIER PENS

Quality pens (before 1945) by these makers are especially desirable:

- Parker (before 1930)
- Montblanc
- Wahl-Eversharp
- Mabie Todd (Swan)
- Waterman
- Dunhill-Namiki
- Sheaffer

1 Pens marked as a calendar with dates and the seven days of the week were only made by Waterman. This was made in 1936 from 9ct gold. £800–1,000

2 The crescent on the side of this *c*.1916 gold-plated Conklin was a new design patented by this US maker in 1899 to improve the way the pen was filled. £300–500

3 This *c*.1905 silver Swan eyedropper is especially valuable because of its high-quality scroll and lozenge decoration. £800–1,200

4 It probably took as long as 2 weeks to decorate this *c*.1935 Dunhill-Namiki pen with such high-quality lacquer decoration. £2,000–3,000

5 The Lily pattern decorating this pen is one of the rarest designs used by Swan during the early years of the 20th century. £1,500–2,000

6 This Montblanc pen, made *c*.1924, is of a fairly standard design, but is still worth £2,000–3,000, because the case is decorated with gold overlay.

7 Although this gold-plated Conklin filigree pen made *c*.1918 is a more common type than No. 2, it's in a larger size and so would still be worth £300–500.

8 There are fakes of this very rare "spider's web" Montblanc Model 1M *c*.1924, but they are usually suspiciously "new" in appearance. £4,000–7,000

9 This "Smallest pen in the World" was a novelty made by Waterman *c*.1910–15; £1,000–1.500. Red versions are much rarer. £5,000–7,000

- Waterman also produced a massive No. 20 safety pen – reputedly used in America for hiding whisky during the Prohibition!

TRIBAL ART

The strong images and primitive shapes which characterize tribal art have enjoyed a huge increase in popularity in recent years. However, because prices have risen steeply and the demand for genuinely old pieces has greatly outstripped supply, there has also been a huge increase in fake pieces on the market. The many fakes produced in Africa and the Far East for the tourist market can be very hard to identify, so if you're an inexperienced collector, buy from a reputable source who can guarantee the age of any piece purporting to be old.

Provenance is fundamental to the value of tribal art. The most desirable pieces are those which have at some time been used for their intended domestic, ceremonial or ritual purpose, and were perhaps collected by colonial settlers or missionaries during the 19th or early 20th century.

WHAT TO LOOK FOR

- Clubs from the Pacific Islands – smaller ones were thrown at enemies to knock them over, larger ones for killing them!
- Maori artefacts with provenance - often faked, so beware.
- North American Indian quillwork and beadwork items.
- .19th century Congo wood figures
- South African snuff containers, pipes, beadwork and carved headrests.

◀ **MASKS**
Masks are one of the most popular collecting areas of tribal art; many were used in tribal festivities and have symbolic significance. This Sepik mask is particularly valuable because of its provenance: it comes from the collection of Frank Wonder who acquired it on an expedition to New Guinea in the 1920s. £5,000–7,000

◀ **CONDITION**
Because of the extreme African climate, wooden objects from before the early 20th century are rare. Such pieces often deteriorate, but a worn patina, as seen on this Urhobo male figure, is desirable and adds to value. £3,000–4,000

▶ **CALABASHES**
The Hawaiian calabash bowl, was a status symbol made from the finest-quality woods, and passed down the

generations within a single family. Before the early 19th century they were usually hand-carved; later examples were made on a lathe. Because the elaborate butterfly repairs on this one actually enhance its aesthetic appeal, it's worth £4,000.

ANTIQUITIES

If, like many collectors, you've always assumed that antiquities are prohibitively expensive, you may be surprised to find out that the average auction of antiquities contains many objects priced at hundreds rather than thousands of pounds. Nonetheless, antiquities have long been sought after, and faking in one form or another has existed throughout the centuries. There is also a further complication in the form of the export laws which exist in most countries where antiquities originate. Collectors should always make sure the piece is being sold legally.

BEWARE

● Antiquities are fragile and condition affects value, but some damage is to be expected – be suspicious of anything which seems too perfect.
● Avoid objects with heavy restoration – particularly if it is on the face of a piece of sculpture or a painting.
● Avoid bronzes which have become badly corroded – their detail may have been irreparably damaged.

▲ EGYPTIAN ANTIQUITIES
Antiquities from ancient Egypt are often extremely valuable. However there are exceptions. This simple redware vase dates from 3,500–3,200 BC and is worth about £300. Other inexpensive antiquities include:
● small Egyptian limestone carvings
● Roman terracotta oil lamps
● small examples of Cypriot pottery.

▼ ROMAN GLASS
It might well seem inconceivable that glass from the 2nd century should be no more expensive than that of the 18th century, but in fact this is often the case. This collection of vases illustrates the subtle colours and iridescence which is typical of much Roman glass and are worth between £300–800 each.

REMEMBER
If you have any doubts about the legality or authenticity of a piece, consult museum experts.

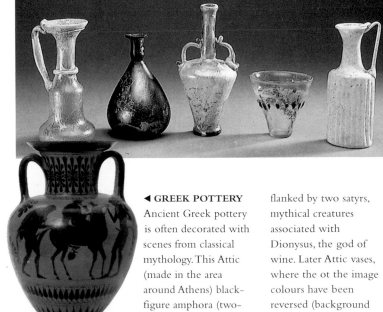

◀ GREEK POTTERY
Ancient Greek pottery is often decorated with scenes from classical mythology. This Attic (made in the area around Athens) black-figure amphora (two-handled urn) dates from c.510–500 BC, and shows a rider flanked by two satyrs, mythical creatures associated with Dionysus, the god of wine. Later Attic vases, where the ot the image colours have been reversed (background black and figures red), are known as red-figure vases. £10,000–15,000

PART 4

FACT FILE

WHERE TO SEE

There is an abundance of places where you can see and study antiques. Some of the major collections to be found in museums and houses open to the public are listed below.

American Museum in Britain
Claverton Manor,
Bath, Avon
Ceramics, Clocks,
Furniture, Silver

Apsley House
Wellington Museum,
149 Piccadilly,
Hyde Park Corner,
London W1
Ceramics, Militaria

Ashmolean Museum
Beaumont Street,
Oxford
Antiquities, Ceramics,
Clocks, Glass, Silver

Attingham Park
Shrewsbury,
Shropshire
Furniture, Silver

Belton House
Grantham, Lincs.
Ceramics, Furniture,
Silver, Textiles

Bethnall Green Museum of Childhood
Cambridge Heath
Road, London, E2
Dolls, Toys

Birmingham City Museum
Chamberlain Square,
Birmingham
Glass

Blenheim Palace
Woodstock, Oxon
Furniture, Silver,
Glass, Ceramics

Blickling Hall
Blickling, Norwich,
Norfolk
Furniture, Textiles

Bristol City Museum and Art Gallery
Queen's Road,
Bristol
Glass

British Museum
Great Russell Street,
Bloomsbury
London WC1
Antiquities, Ceramics,
Clocks, Glass,
Silver

Burghley House
Stamford,
Northants
Furniture

The Burrel Collection
Pollock Country
Park,
Glasgow
Antiquities,
Decorative Arts,
Oriental Arts

Castle Museum and Nottingham Art Gallery
Nottingham
Ceramics

Castle Museum
Tower Street,
York
Ceramics, Silver,
Sheffield Plate

Cecil Higgins Art Gallery and Museum
Castle Close,
Bedford
Ceramics, Glass

Clandon Park
West Clandon,
Guildford
Ceramics, Furniture,
Textiles

Cutler's Company
Cutler's Hall,
Church Street,
Sheffield
Silver, Sheffield Plate

Derby Museum & Art Gallery
The Strand,
Derby
Porcelain

Dyson Perrins Museum
Seven Street,
Worcester
Ceramics

Felbrigg Hall
Norwich,
Norfolk
Furniture

Fenton House
Windmill Hill,
Hampstead,
London NW3

Ceramics,
Furniture

Fitzwilliam Museum
Trumptinton Street,
Cambridge
Ceramics,
Clocks, Glass

Geffrye Museum
Kingsland Road,
London E2
Furniture,
Decorative Arts

Glasgow Art Gallery & Museum
Kelvingrove,
Glasgow
Ceramics, Silver

Greyfrairs
Friar Street,
Worcester
Furniture, Textiles

Gunby Hall
Gunby,
Near Spilsby,
Lincolnshire
Furniture

Ham House
Richmond,
Surrey
Furniture

Hampton Court Palace
Hampton,
Middlesex
Ceramics, Furniture,
Rugs, Textiles

Harewood House
Leeds,
West Yorkshire
Furniture

Ickworth
The Rotunda,
Horringer,
Bury St Edmunds
Furniture, Silver

**Imperial War
Museum**
Lambeth Road,
London SE1
Armour, Arms

Jewel House
Tower of London
London EC3
Silver, Metalware

Knole
Sevenoaks,
Kent
*Carpets, Ceramics,
Furniture, Textiles*

**Laing Art Gallery
and Museum**
Higham Place,
Newcastle
Ceramics, Glass

**Lady Lever
Art Gallery**
Port Sunlight,
Merseyside
Furniture

Longleat House
Warminster,
Wilts
Ceramics, Furniture

**Manchester City
Art Gallery**
Mosley Street,
Manchester
Glass

Montacute House
Montacute,

Somerset
(early April-end Sept)
Furniture, Textiles

**National Maritime
Museum**
Romney Road,
Greenwich,
London SE10
*Navigational and
Scientific Instruments*

**National Museum
of Ireland**
Kildare Street and
Marrion Street
Dublin
Glass, Silver

**National Museum
of Scotland**
Chambers Street,
Edinburgh
*Ceramics, Decorative Arts,
Silver*

Petworth House
Petworth,
Sussex
Furniture, Sculpture

**Pilkington Glass
Museum**
Pilkington Bros. Ltd.,
Prescot Road,
St Helens,
Merseyside
Glass

Osterley Park
Isleworth,
Middlesex
Ceramics, Furniture

Polesden Lacy
Dorking, Surrey
*Ceramics, Furniture,
Photographs, Silver*

Royal Pavilion
Brighton,
Sussex
*Ceramics, Furniture,
Glass, Rugs,
Textiles*

Rufford Old Hall
Rufford,
Ormskirk,
Lancashire
*Armour, Arms,
Furniture, Textiles*

**The Science
Museum**
Exhibition Road,
London SW7
*Barometers, Scientific
Instruments*

**Sheffield City
Museum**
Weston Park,
Sheffield
Sheffield Plate

Shugborough
Milford,
Near Stafford,
Staffordshire
*Ceramics,
Furniture, Silver*

Standen
East Grinstead,
Sussex
*Art Nouveau
Ceramics, Furniture,
Textiles*

**Stoke-on-Trent
City Museum
and Art Gallery**
Broad Street,
Hanley,
Stoke-on-Trent
Ceramics

Syon House
Brentford,
Middlesex
Clocks

Tatton Park
Knutsford, Cheshire
*Ceramics, Furniture,
Glass, Silver*

**Temple
Newsam House**
Leeds
*Ceramics,
Furniture, Silver*

**Victoria and
Albert Museum**
Cromwell Road,
London SW1
*Art Nouveau,
Ceramics, Clocks,
Furniture, Glass,
Rugs and Carpets,
Silver, Textiles*

Waddesdon Manor
Aylesbury, Bucks.
*Carpets, Ceramics,
Furniture*

Wallace Collection
Hertford House,
Manchester Square,
London W1
*Ceramics, Furniture,
Silver*

Windsor Castle
Windsor, Berkshire
*Ceramics, Clocks,
Furniture, Rugs*

**Worcester Porcelain
Museum**
Severn Street,
Worcester
Ceramics

WHERE TO BUY

MAJOR AUCTION HOUSES

Bearnes
Rainbow,
Avenue Road,
Torquay,
Devon
Tel 01803 296277

Bonhams
Montpelier Street,
London, SW7
Tel 020 7393 3900

Christie's
8 King Street,
St James's,
London SW1
Tel 020 7839 9060

Henry Spencer & Son
20 The Square,
Retford,
Notts.
Tel 0115 950 8833

Lawrences of Crewkerne
South Street,
Crewkerne,
Somerset
Tel 01460 73041

Lots Road Auction Galleries
71 Lots Road,
Brompton
London SW10
Tel 020 7376 6800

Outhwaite & Litherland
Kingsway Galleries,
Fontenoy Street,
Liverpool
Tel 0151 236 6561

Phillips
Blenstock House,
101 New Bond Street,
London W1
Tel 020 7629 6602

Rosebery's Fine Art
74 Knights Hill
London SE19
Tel 020 8761 2522

Sotheby's
34–35 New Bond Street,
London W1
Tel 020 7293 5000

MAJOR ANTIQUES FAIRS

JANUARY
London Ceramics Fair
Cumberland Hotel,
Marble Arch,
London W1
Tel 0870 400 8701

The LAPADA Antiques and Fine Art Fair
National Exhibition Centre,
Birmingham
Tel 0121 780 4141

West London Antiques and Fine Art Fair
Kensington Town Hall,
Hornton Street ,
London W8
Tel 01444 482514

Westminster Antiques Fair
The Royal Horticultural Hall,
Vincent Square,
London SW1
Tel 020 7254 4054

FEBRUARY
Harrogate Winter Antiques Fair
Pavilions of Harrogate,
North Yorkshire
Tel 01277 214677

London Antique Dealers' Fair
Café Royal,
Regent Street,
London W1
Tel 0672 870727

MARCH
The British Antique Dealers Association Fair
The Duke of York's Headquarters,
Chelsea,
London SW3
Tel 020 7586 6108

The Chelsea Antiques Fair
Old Town Hall,
King's Road,
London SW3
Tel 01444 482514

Cheshire County Antiques Fair
Arley Hall,
Near Knutsford,
Cheshire
Tel 01249 661111

Lancashire Spring AntiquesFair
Hoghton Tower,
Hoghton,
Near Preston,
Lancs.ashire
Tel 01277 214677

Wilton House Antiques Fair
Wilton House,
Wilton,
Near Salisbury,
Wiltshire
Tel 01722 743115

APRIL
Antiques for Everyone
National Exhibition Centre,
Birmingham
Tel 0121 780 4141

Thames Valley Antiques Dealers Association Antiques Fair
The Blue Coat School,
Holme Park,
Sonning-On-Thames,
Berkshire
Tel 01865 341639

MAY
Antiques Fair
Alnwick Castle,
Northumberland,
Tel 01423 522122

Buxton Antiques Fair
The Pavilion Gardens,
Buxton,
Derbyshire
Tel 01483 422562

The Antique Dealers Fair of Wales
The Orangery,
Margam Park,
Port Talbot,
South Wales
Tel 01202 604306

JUNE
Antiquarian Book Fair
Olympia 2,
London W1
Tel 020 7439 3118

Summer Olympia Fine Art and Antiques Fair
Olympia,
London SW1
Tel 020 7370 8212

Grosvenor House Art and Antiques Fair
Grosvenor House Hotel,
London W1
Tel 020 7495 8743

The International Ceramics Fair
Park Lane Hotel,
Piccadilly,
London W1
Tel 020 7734 5491

AUGUST
Kensington Antiques Fair
Kensington Town Hall,
Hornton Street,
London
Tel 01444 482514

SEPTEMBER
Irish Antique Dealers Fair
Royal Dublin Society,
Ballsbridge,
Dublin
Tel 01 2859294

Stafford Antiques Fair
Stafford Bingley Hall,
County Showground,
Stafford
Tel 07071 284333

OCTOBER
Chester Antiques Fair
County Grandstand,
Chester Racecourse
Tel 01444 482514

Surrey Antiques Fair
Civic Hall,
8 Meadow Road
Godalming,
Surrey
Tel 01483 422562

NOVEMBER
Olympia Antiques Fair
The Grand Hall,
Olympia 2,
London W1
Tel 020 7370 8188

Hertfordshire Antiques Fair
Hatfield House,
Hatfield Park,
Hertfordshire
Tel 01277 214699

DECEMBER
Newark International Antiques and Collectors Fair
Newark and Nottinghamshire Showground,
Newark-On-Trent,
Nottinghamshire
Tel 01636 702326

Wembley Antiques and Collectors Fair
Wembley Exhibition Centre,
Near Wembley Stadium,
London NW2
01636 702326

ANTIQUES MARKETS

Alfie's Antiques Market
13-25 Church Street,
London W1
Tel 020 7723 6066
(Tuesday-Saturday)

Antiquarius
King's Road,
London SW3
Tel 020 7351 5353
(Monday-Saturday)

Bath Antiques Market
Guinea Lane,
Landsdown Road,
Bath,
Avon
Tel 020 7351 5353
(Wednesdays)

Bermondsey Market
Bermondsey Street,
London SE1
Tel 020 7351 5353
(Friday from 5 a.m.)

Camden Passage
Islington,
London N1
Tel 020 7 359 0190
(Tuesday-Saturday)

Chenil Galleries
King's Road,
Chelsea,
London SW3
Tel 020 7351 5829
(Monday-Saturday)

Cloisters Antiques Fairs
St Andrews Hall,
Norwich,
Norfolk
Tel 01603 628477
(Wednesdays)

Grey's Antique Market
Davies Street,
London W1
Tel 020 7629 7034
(Monday-Friday) ·

Great Western Antique Centre
Bartlett Street,
Bath,
Avon
Tel 01225 424243

Portobello Road Antiques Market
Portobello Road,
London W11
(Saturdays)

Preston Antique Centre
New Hall Lane,
Preston,
Lancashire
Tel 01772 794498
(Monday-Sunday)

Taunton Silver Street Antiques
27-29 Silver Street,
Taunton,
Somerset
Tel 01823 289327
(Mondays)

The Antique Centre
56 Garstang Road,
Preston,
Lancashire
Tel 01772 882078
(Monday-Sunday)

The Lanes
Brighton,
East Sussex
(Monday-Saturday)

Woburn Abbey Antiques Centre
Woburn Abbey,
Woburn,
Bedfordshire
Tel 01525 290350
(Monday-Sunday)

DEALERS' ASSOCIATIONS

British Antique Dealers' Association (BADA)
20 Rutland Gate,
London SW7
Tel 020 7589 4128

London and Provincial Antique Dealers' Association (LAPADA)
535 Kings Road,
London SW10
Tel 020 7823 3511

WHAT TO READ

General

Bly, John, *Is it Genuine?* (1986)

Collins, *Encylopedia of Antiques* (1973)

Fleming, John, and Honour, Hugh, *The Penguin Dictionary of Decorative Arts* (1977)

Hughes, Therle, *The Country Life Antiques Handbook* (1986)

Miller, Martin and Judith, *Miller's Antiques Price Guide* (1992)

Miller's Pocket Antiques Fact File (1988)

Miller's Pocket Dictionary of Antiques (1990)

Miller's Understanding Antiques (1989)

Osborne, Harold, *Oxford Companion to the Decorative Arts* (1985)

Savage, George, *Dictionary of Antiques* (1970)

Simpson, M., and Huntley, M. (Ed.), *Sotheby's Caring for Antiques* (1992)

Furniture

Aguis, Pauline, *British Furniture 1880–1915* (1978)

Aslin, Elizabeth, *Nineteenth Century English Furniture* (1962)

Bly, John, *Discovering English Furniture* (1976)

Chinnery, Victory, *Oak Furniture - The British Tradition* (1979)

Collard, Frances, *Regency Furniture* (1983)

Comstock, Helen, *Victorian Furniture and Windsor Chairs* (1958)

Edwards, R., *Shorter Dictionary of English Furniture* (1964)

Edwards, R., and Jourdain, M., *Georgian Cabinet-Makers* (1955)

Hayward, Helena, *World Furniture* (1965)

Jervis, Simon, *Victorian Furniture* (1968)

Joy, Edward T., *English Furniture 1800–1851* (1977)

Miller, Martin and Judith , *Miller's Antiques Checklist – Furniture* (1991)

Payne, Christopher, *19th Century European Furniture* (1985)

(Ed.) *Sotheby's Concise Encylcopedia of Furniture* (1989)

Symonds, W.R. and Whinneray, B.B., *Victorian Furniture* (1978)

Ceramics

Atterbury, Paul, *History of Porcelain* (1982)

Battie, David and Turner, Michael, *The Price Guide to 19th & 20th Century Pottery*

Charleston, Robert (Ed.), *World Ceramics* (1981)

Godden, G.A., *Eighteenth Century English Porcelain* (1985)

Encyclopedia of British Pottery & Porcelain Manufacturers (1988)

Illustrated Encylopedia of British Pottery and Porcelain (1992)

Oriental Export Market Porcelains (1979)

Staffordshire Porcelain (1983)

Halfpenny, Pat, *English Earthenware Figures 1740–1840* (1992)

Hillier, Bevis, *Pottery and Porcelain 1700–1914* (1968)

Honey, W.B., *French Porcelain of the 18th Century* (1950)

Hughes, Bernard and Therle, *English Porcelain and Bone China, 1743–1850* (1955)

Jenyns, Soame, *Japanese Porcelain* (1985)

Medley, Margaret, *The Art of the Chinese Potter* (1981)

Morley-Fletcher, Hugo, *Meissen* (1971)

Oliver, Anthony, *Staffordshire Pottery The Tribal Art of England* (1981)

Savage, George, *Porcelain Through the Ages* (1954)

Saville, Rosalind, *Sèvres Porcelain* (1980)

Sato, M., *Chinese Ceramics, A Short History* (1981)

Sotheby's, *Concise Encylopedia of Porcelain* (1990)

Thomas, E. Lloyd, *Victorian Pottery* (1974)

Williams-Wood, Cyril, *Staffordshire Pot Lids and Their Potters* (1972)

Glass

Bickerton, L., *18th Century English Drinking Glasses* (1986)

Dodsworth, Roger, *Glass and Glassmakers* (1982)

Grover, Ray and Lee, *Art Nouveau Glass* (1967)

Hajdamach, C., *British & European 19th Century Glass*

Mackay, James, *Glass Paperweights* (1973)

O'Looney, Betty, *Victorian Glass* (1972)

Slack, R., *English Pressed Glass* (1987)

Sotheby's Concise Encylopedia of Glass (1991)

Wakefield, Hugh, *Nineteenth Century British Glass* (1961)

Silver & Gold

Bradbury, Frederick, *Bradbury's Book of Hallmarks* (1975)

History of Old Sheffield Plate (1968)

Brett, Vanessa, *Sotheby's Directory of Silver* (1986)

Bury, Shirley, *Victorian Electroplate* (1971)

Clayton, Michael, *The Collector's Dictionary of Gold and Silver* (1985)

Culme, J.,
Directory of Gold &
Silversmiths 1938 1914
(1987)
Grimwade, Arthur,
London Goldsmiths
1697 1837
(1976)
Hughes, G. Bernard,
Small Antique Silverware
(including flatware)
(1971)
Jackson, Charles,
English Goldsmiths and
Their Marks (1921)
Pickford, I.,
Silver Flatware
Sotheby's Concise
Encyclopedia of Silver
(1991)
Waldron, Peter,
Price Guide to Antique
Silver (1982)

Carpets & Textiles
Bennett, Ian,
Rugs and Carpets of the
World (1977)
Black, David (Ed.),
World Rugs and
Carpets (1985)
Edwards, A. Cecil,
The Persian Carpet
(1953)
Eiland, Murray,
Oriental Rugs, A
Comprehensive
Guide (1976)

Ford, P.R.J.,
Oriental Carpet
Design
Franses, Jack,
European and Oriental
Rugs (1970)
Godden, G.A.,
Stevenographs and
Victorian Silk Pictures
(1971)
Hughes, Therele,
English Domestic
Needlework (1961)
Middleton,, Andrew
Rugs and Carpets (1996)

Clocks
Bird, A.,
English House Clocks
1600 1850 (1873)
Britten, F.J., Britten's
Watch and Clockmakers
Handbook (1982)
Bruton, Eric,
Antique Clocks and
Clock Collecting
(1974)
Cescinskey, Herbert,
and Webster, Malcolm
R., *English Domestic*
Clocks (176)
Loomes, Brian,
Early Clockmakers of
Great Britain (1981)
Miller, Martin and
Judith (Ed.), *Miller's*
Antiques Checklist –
Clocks (1992)

Art Nouveau/
Art Deco
Arwas, Victor,
Art Deco (1980)
Dawes, Nicholas, M.,
Lalique Glass (1986)
Garner, Philippe (Ed.),
Phaidon Encyclopedia
of Decorative Arts
1890–1940 (1978)
Hillier, Bevis,
Posters (1969)
The World of Art Deco
(1971)
Miller, Martin and
Judith (Ed.), *Miller's*
Antiques Checklist – Art
Deco (1991)
Miller's Antiques
Checklist – Art Nouveau
(1992)

Bears, Dolls & Toys
Ayres, W.S.,
The Main Street Pocket
Guide to Toys (1981)
Brewster, K., and
Waugh, R., *The Official*
Price Guide to Antique
and Modern Teddy Bears
(1988)
Coleman, E.A.D.,
and E.J., *The Collector's*
Encyclopedia of Dolls
Vol I & II (1968)
Darbyshire, E. (Ed.),
The Collectors'
Encyclopedia of Toys

and Dolls (1990)
King, C.E.,
The Encyclopedia of Toys
(1978)
Miller, Martin and
Judith (Ed.), *Miller's*
Antiques Checklist –
Dolls and Teddy Bears
(1992)
Schoonmaker, P.,
The Collector's History of
the Teddy Bear (1981)
Taylor, Kerry, Letts
Guide to Collecting Dolls
(1990)

Other Collectables
Baddiel, Sarah Fabian,
The World of Golf
Collectables (1992)
Kay, Hilary, *Rock and*
Roll Collectables (1992)
Kewley Charles & J.
Howard Farrar,
Fishing Tackle for
Collectors (1989)
Lambrou, Andreas,
Fountain Pens Vintage
& Modern (1989)
Rolley, Claude,
Greek Bronzes (1986)
Turner, Anthony, *Early*
Scientific Instruments
(1987)
Turner, Gerard, L.E.,
Nineteenth Century
Scientific Instruments
(1983)

GLOSSARY

Acanthus Decorative leaf motif used to adorn a wide variety of objects.

Acid cutting A method of decorating glass where objects were coated with an acid-resistant substance, such as wax; a design was scratched on the wax with a steel point and fixed by dipping the object in acid.

Air twist stem On drinking glasses and other glassware, a stem decorated with spiral filaments of hollow glass.

Albarello (-i) A tin-glazed drug jar with a narrow waist.

Ambrotype A photograph made by exposing a glass plate treated with light-sensitive wet collodion. The negative was made positive by backing with black paper or paint (see p150).

Appliqué In textiles, applying small patches of fabric to a base fabric to make a design.

Arita An important centre for Japanese porcelain production, and a term used to describe one distinctive type of Japanese porcelain made in the area (see p67).

Armorial An engraved design showing a crest or coat of arms.

Arts & Crafts A late 19th century artistic movement led by William Morris which advocated a return to medieval standards of craftsmanship and simplicity of design.

Automata A term covering a wide variety of mechanical toys with moving parts, popular during the 18th and 19th centuries.

Baluster Vase-shaped form with a bulbous base, narrow waist and slightly flared neck. Commonly used on silverwares, ceramics and stems of drinking glasses.

Ball and claw A furniture foot in the shape of an animal's paw grasping on ball. Used on cabriole legs.

Basaltes Unglazed black stoneware, developed by Wedgwood.

Bergère French-style armchair with wood frame and upholstered sides.

Berlin Woolwork Amateur embroidery using coloured wools on a canvas grid.

Biscuit Unglazed porcelain, fired only once.

Blue-dash charger A delftware dish decorated with a border of blue brush strokes.

Blueing A decorative heat treatment applied to metal weapons which also protect from rust.

Bone china Porcelain made by the addition of large quantities of bone ash.

Bracket clock A type of spring-driven clock, designed to stand on a surface.

Britannia metal An alloy of tin antimony and copper, used during the 19th century as a substitute for pewter.

Cabriole leg A furniture leg in the shape of an elongated S.

Cameo glass Wares made by combining two or more layers of differently coloured glass which was carved to make a design in relief.

Carriage clock A small portable clock with a carrying handle (see p110).

Case furniture Furniture intended as a receptacle, such as a chest of drawers.

Chasing A method of decorating silver and other metals by creating a raised pattern using a hammer or punch. Also known as embossing.

Chinoiserie Oriental-style fixtures and scenes used to decorate many different types of object.

Creamware Creamy-white earthenware.

Cornice The projecting moulding at the top of tall pieces of furniture.

Credenza A long side-cabinet with glazed or solid doors.

Cross-banding A veneered edge at right-angles to the main veneer.

Cruet A frame for holding casters and bottles containing condiments.

Davenport A small writing desk with a sloped top above a case of drawers.

Delftware Tin-glazed earthenware from England or the Low Countries.

Dial The "face" of a clock, which shows the time.

Distressed A term used to describe an object that has been artificially aged.

Drum table A circular-topped table with a frieze containing drawers and supported by a central pedestal.

Ebonized Stained black in imitation of ebony.

Étui A small case for scissors and other small implements.

Faïence Tin-glazed earthenware from France.

Façon de Venise Glassware imitating Venetian styles.

Flatback Ceramic portrait figures with flat, undecorated backs, designed to stand against a wall or on a mantelpiece (see p81)

Flatware Any flat or shallow tableware, such as plates or cutlery.

Gesso A plaster-like substance use as a substitute for carved wood, or as a base for painted or gilded decoration.

Hallmark The marks stamped on silver or gold objects when passed at assay (the test for quality).

Hard-paste porcelain Porcelain made using the ancient Chinese combination of kaolin and petuntse.

Imari A type of Japanese porcelain with opulent decoration inspired by brocade designs, exported through the port of Imari.

Intaglio Incised gemstone or any incised decoration; the opposite of carving in relief.

Istoriato Narrative scenes painted on Italian *maiolica*.

Jacobite glass Wine glasses engraved with symbols of the Jacobites (supporters of Prince Charles Edward

Stuart's claim to the throne).

Japanning European imitation of Oriental lacquer (see p58).

Jasperware A hard fine-grained stoneware decorated with high relief medallions, developed by Wedgwood.

Joined Term used to describe furniture made by a joiner.

Kakeimon Sparsely-decorated Japanese porcelain made by the Kakiemon family in the 17th century. The style was much imitated by later potters.

Kaolin A fine white granite clay used in hard-paste porcelain, also known as China clay.

Kashan Rug-making centre in Southern Iran, noted for high quality products.

Kazak Rugs from central Caucaus, usually decorated with distinctive geometric designs.

Kelim A flat woven Persian rug (made with no pile).

Kneehole desk A writing desk with drawers on either side and a central recess for the user's legs.

Ladder back A country chair with a back made from a series of horizontal bars

between the two vertical uprights.

Ladik A Turkish prayer rug, usually decorated with a niche and stylized tulip flowers.

Lap joint In silverware, the technique used to join a spoon finial to the stem by cutting each piece in opposing L-shapes.

Lead Crystal Glass containing lead oxide which gives extra weight and brilliance.

Library table A rectangular table with frieze drawers, end supports and a central stretcher.

Linen chest A hybrid coffer/chest of drawers, which may have both drawers and a lift-up top.

Loaded In silverware, a hollow object (often a candlestick) which has been filled with pitch and a metal rod to give weight.

Lock The firing mechanism of a gun.

Long arm A firearm with a long barrel.

Longcase clock A tall clock with a case containing weights and pendulum and hood housing dial and movement.

Lowboy A small dressing table, often with a single frieze drawer flanked by a deeper drawer.

Maiolica Tin-glazed earthenwares from Italy.

Majolica Enamelled stoneware with high relief decoration developed by Minton in the 19th century.

Marquetry Design formed from veneers of differently coloured woods.

Marriage The joining together of two previously unrelated parts to form a whole.

Mihrab A niche with a pointed arch, seen on prayer rugs.

Millefiori Glass made by fusing differently coloured rods of glass which resembles "a thousand flowers"; used especially for paperweights.

Monteith Large silver bowl, with a shallow scalloped rim.

Mortise and tenon Type of joint used in furniture; the mortise is a cavity, into which the shaped tenon fits and is held in place by dowels.

Mother-of-pearl Slices of shell often used for decorative inlay.

Motif A decorative detail, often repeated to form a pattern.

Moulded glass 19th century glasswares manufactured in large quantities by forcing glass into a mould.

Mystery clock A clock of novel form in which the movement is ingeniously disguised.

Nailsea A factory near Bristol famous for novelty glass objects.

Occasional table Small, easily portable table.

Octant Device made from one-eighth of a circle, used for measuring angular distance.

Opaque twist A white or coloured twist of glass contained within the stem of a drinking glass.

Ormolu Gilded bronze or brass; term also sometimes loosely used to describe any yellow-coloured metal.

Overglaze A second glaze laid over a first and refired; also known as enamelling.

Pad foot On furniture a rounded foot, resembling that of an animal.

Palmette A stylized palm-leaf motif, often used to decorate Oriental carpets and furniture.

Papier mâché Paper pulp combined with glue, used to make small objects such as boxes and trays; also applied over a metal frame to make larger pieces of furniture, such as tables and chairs.

Parcel gilt Wood that has been partly gilded.

Parian Fine white biscuit porcelain resembling marble; popular from mid-19th century.

Parquetry Decorative veneers of wood laid in a geometric pattern.

Pate The crown of a doll's head.

Patina The term used to describe the surface colour and sheen of furniture and silver which is built up from years of use and careful polishing.

Petuntse China stone; a granite used to make hard paste porcelain.

Plate A generic term for gold and silver vessels, not to be confused with Sheffield Plate or plated wares.

Porringer A two-handled dish sometimes with a lid, originally for holding porridge or broth. Made from silver and pewter.

Pressed glass 19th century glasswares formed by mechanical pressure applied to molten glass in a mould.
see also Moulded glass

Quadrant A quarter circle, marked with degrees of a circle and with a weighted line or pointer, used as a navigational aid.

Quarter-veneered Four pieces of identical veneer, which are laid opposite each other to create a decorative effect.

Quartetto tables A set of four graduating matching tables, that can be stored inside each other.

Rack The structure, comprising several shelves, at the top of some dressers.

Raised work Type of embroidery which incorporates areas of decoration raised up with padding – also called stumpwork

Refectory table Term used to describe the long rectangular dining tables of the 17th century and later.

Reproduction A piece which is a copy of an early design.

"Right" Dealers' term for something which is genuine and authentic as opposed to "wrong", which means it is faked, altered or restored.

Sabre A curving sword used mainly by cavalrymen.

Sabre leg An elegant outward curving leg, associated with Regency furniture.

Salt A dish or cellar designed for holding salt.

Sampler Needlework pictures; incorporating different stitches and designs.

Scent bottle A small portable flask, often flattened pear shape.

Sconce A plate or bracket on the wall to which lights or candle-holders could be attached. Also used to describe the wall lights themselves.

Settle A long wooden seat with a back and arms, and possibly a box seat.

Sextant Navigational instruments, formed from one-sixth of a circle.

Sgrafitto Decorative techinque whereby the surface has been scratched or incised to show a contrasting colour beneath; used mainly on ceramics and glass.

Shako A 19th century military cap of conical shape with a peak.

Shiraz Centre of distribution in central Iran for nomadic rugs decorated with simple geometric designs.

Slip Clay mixed with water, often used to decorate pottery.

Snuffer Cone-shaped metal implement used to extinguish candles.

Sterling silver Silver of at least 925 parts per 1000 purity. The minimum standard for English silver.

Stock The wooden part of a firearm to which the metal barrel and firing mechanism are attached.

Tester The wooden canopy over a bed, it may cover only half the bed and be supported by two or four posts; hence full tester or half tester beds.

Train A set of cog wheels and pinions in a clock movement.

Treen Small wooden domestic objects, sometimes in the shape of fruit.

Tunbridge ware Objects decorated with pictures or designs made from bundles of differently coloured wood cut in sections.

Tureen A large bowl on a foot used for serving soup.

Turned furniture Pieces made by turning on a lathe.

Veneer A thin sheet of wood applied to furniture for decorative effect.

Vesta case A small box used to contain vestas – early matches.

Vinaigrette A small portable container containing a sponge scented with vinegar.

Warp Threads used to make the foundation of a carpet running from one end of the carpet to the other and form the fringes.

Weft Cross-wise threads, which run at right angles to the warp in any woven textiles.

Wet plate camera Earliest form of camera, often made from brass-bound mahogany.

Whatnot Tall stand of four or five display shelves and sometimes a drawer in the base.

Windsor chair Country chair, usually with a saddle seat, hoop back and simple turned legs.

Wine funnel Cone, with a spout and often a matching fish for filtering and decanting wine.

Wing chair Upholstered chair with a high back and wing-like side projections.

X-frame The X-shaped construction of some chairs and stools.

INDEX

ACKNOWLEDGMENTS

The publishers would like to thank the following auction houses, museums, dealers, collectors and other sources for supplying pictures for use in this book.

Front jacket tlSPL,tclOPG,trOPG,cCI,blCI,brOPG/Mark West; **front jacket flap** OPG/SuePearson; **back jacket** OPG/Juliette Edwards
2vaseSL, spoonCS, figuresCL, paperweightCL, longcaseSL, shoesCNY, clockSL, faseSL, tobyjugCSK, chairSL, tureenSL, bureauCL, rugSL; 3bowlSK, trainsCSK, dollSL, casterSL, stoolSL, glassCL;
10P;**11**SL;**12**CSK;**13**tCSK,bB;**14**B;**15**B;**16**L;**17**AP;**18**P;**19**P;**20**NEC;**21**P;**22**tP,blBY,brP;**26**KSA;**27**CC;**28**B;**29**B;
32DS;**34**WD;**35**SR;**36**SP;**37**CL;**41**OPG;**42**SL,bWG;**43**JGM;**44**SL;**45**tSL,bLG;**46**rWB;**47**tlWB,Hum,blWB,brLB;
50PJ;**51**cRen,bWB;**52**SL;**53**tOPG,ctW,cbJGM,bHum;**54**tlSL,rtSL,clSL,blSL;**55**SL;**56**bWB;**57**tWil,cSL,bHock;**58** blRD,rSL;**59**blLB,rSL;**60**tlCL,clWak;**61**lSL,cWB,bCL;**62**S;**63**lCL,rCL;**65**tCL;**66**SL,blSL,brCSK;**67**cSL,brSL;**68**l CNY,cSL,rCNY;**69**lCL,BSL,rCL;**70**blSL;**71**SL;**72**lSL,rCL,bcSL;**73**tSL,crSZ;**74**clCL,crSL,bCL;**75**tx2SL;**76**tCL,b SL;**77**CL;**78**CKS;**79**cOPG;**80**tOPG,cLS,bSNY;**81**lSL,cOPG,rDen;**84**tlCNY,cCNY,bcCNY;**85**SLx2;**86**lCL,rCNY;
87tSL,clCNY,crCNY;**88**cSL,blCNY,cbSL,rbSK;**89**CNY;**90**ctSL,clCL,bSL;**91**cSL,crCNY,blCNY;**92**cSKx3,bcOPG;
93CNYx3;**94**lSB,rCL;**95**tlSL,cSB,bC;**96**CL;**97**clCL,crSL;**98**lCL,rSL;**99**SLx2;**100**CL;**101**tlH&G,crSL,bSL;**102**SLx 2,bcCL;**103**SL,bx3CNY;**106**lSL,ctSO,crSL;**107**SO;**108**cAW,crLS;**109**SL;**110**SLx3;**111**lCL,rSL,brDR;**113**lSNY, rSNY,bSNY;**114**lCL,rCL;**115**lCL,rCL,bSL;**116**lx2;**117**cSL,bSNY;**118**tCL,bSL;**119**tlCL,trPS,bCL;**120**lSL,rCNY, rbCNY;**121**Bx5;**122**lSL,rRC,bCL;**123**cCL,bCL;**124**trSL,clSL,crCL;**125**lCNY,cCL,rCNY;**126**SL;**127**lSL,rPC,bB;
128lSLx2,bPS;**129**cCSK,bSNY;**131**lSL,clCSK,crLS,rCKS;**132**SLx2;**133**cSP,bSL;**134**SPx3;**135**cSP,bDA;**136**CL;**137** rCL,cCL,bMaB;**138**tSL,cCSK,bSL;**139**rSL,cCNY;**140**CKS;**141**CSKx3;**142**CSKx2,bSL;**143**CSKx3;**144**SL;**145** tCNY,cSL,bWAL;**146**lSL,rSL;**147**rPS,cCL,bPS;**148**CLx3;**149**CLx3;**150**OPG;**151**CSKx3;**152**cSKx2;**153**CSKx4;
154SBx2;**155**t&cSP,bSNY;**156**l,c,rCSK,blSL;**157**B;**158**brB,trCL;**159**cl,crCSK,bSL;**160**BY

Key

t top, **c** centre, **b** bottom, **l** left, **r** right
AP Adrian Stemp Antiques, Brighton; **AW** Anthony Woodburn, Leigh, Kent; **B** Bonhams; **BY** Bermondsey Market; **CC** The Clock Clinic, Lower Richmond Rd; London; **CI** Christie's Images; **CL** Christie's London; **CNY** Christie's New York; **CS** Christie's Scotland; **CSK** Christie's South Kensington; **DA** Dottie Ayres; **Den** Richard Dennis, Ilminster; **DR** Derek Roberts, Tonbridge, Kent; **DS** Dennis Severs, Folgate Street, London; **H&G** Hope and Glory, Kensington Church Street, London; **Hock** William Hockley Antiques, Petworth, West Sussex; **Hum** Humphrey Antiques, Petworth, West Sussex; **JGM** John G Morris Ltd., Petworth; **KSA** Keith Skeel Antiques, Islington High Street, London; **LB** Lesley Bragge Antiques, Petworth, West Sussex; **MaB** Mint and Boxed, London; **NEC** British International Antiques Fair, Birmingham; **OPG** Octopus Publishing Group Ltd: **P** Portobello Road; **PC** Phillips, Cardiff; **PJ** Patrick Jefferson Antiques, London; **PS** Philips, London; **RC** Royal Copenhagen; **RD** Richard Davidson Antiques, Arundel, West Sussex; **Ren** Rendall Antiques, London; **SB** Sotheby's, Billingshurst; **SL** Sotheby's London; **SNY** Sotheby's New York; **SO** Strike One, Balcombe Street, London; **SP** Sue Pearson Antiques, Brighton; **SPL** Sotheby's Picture Library; **SR** Sotheby's Restoration Department; **SZ** Sotheby's Zurich; **Wak** Michael Wakelin and Helen Linfield, Petworth, West Sussex; **WAL** Wallis & Wallis, Lewes, Sussex; **WB** William Bedford plc, London; **WD** West Dean College, West Sussex; **Wil** T.G. Wilkinson Antiques, Petworth, West Sussex

Special photography by Ian Booth, Jacqui Hurst, A. J. Photographics and Tim Ridley.
Illustrations by Karen Cochrane, Simon Miller, John Hutchinson and Vanessa Luff

The publishers would also like to thank the following specialists for their help in the preparation of this book:
Furniture Richard Davidson **Pottery and Porcelain** Gordon Lang, Eric Knowles **Silver and Metalware** John Wilson **Glass** Eric Knowles **Clocks** John Mighell **Rugs and Carpets; Textiles** Joanna Macfarlane **Art Nouveau and Art Deco** Eric Knowles **Dolls and Bears** Sue Pearson **Rock and Pop, Films** Carey Wallace **Other Collectables** Alex Crum-Ewing **Tribal** Kevin Conru
Special thanks are are also due to the following for their help in updating this edition:
Daniel Agrew, Graham Budd, Alexander Crum-Ewing, Karin Dobbin, Leslie Gillham, Eric Knowles, Stephen Maycock, John Mighell, Sue Pearson, Siobahn Quin, Christopher Spencer, Alison Toplis, John Wilson